LOVE, SEX, AND FRIENDSHIP

in no particular order

www.mascotbooks.com

Love, Sex, and Friendship: In No Particular Order

I have tried to recreate events, locales and conversations from my memories of them. In order to maintain their anonymity, in some instances I have changed the names of individuals and places, I may have changed some identifying characteristics and details such as physical properties, occupations, and places of residence.

For more information, please contact:
Mascot Books
620 Herndon Parkway, Suite 320
Herndon, VA 20170
info@mascotbooks.com

Library of Congress Control Number: 2019905401

CPSIA Code: PBANG1019A
ISBN-13: 978-1-64307-348-4

Printed in the United States

This book is dedicated to the two adult loves of my life:
The type of best friend every woman deserves and
the type of husband every woman wishes for.

LOVE, SEX, AND FRIENDSHIP

in no particular order

FARISSA KNOX

Kate,
Loved meeting
you and twinning
in our CK
dresses ♡

[signature]

Contents

Introduction

"Which one do you think wears the strap-on when they are having their lesbian sex?"

This is how random Tuesday morning conversations used to start for my best friend and I when we walked into work most mornings. Of course, this was after I had made a cup of coffee, checked my e-mail, and read my and my boyfriend's horoscope. Ayesha and I met at work in 2005. We were both account executives at a national radio rep firm that sold advertising for a number of radio stations across the country.

Believe me, it sounds much more exciting than it really was.

In reality, we were responsible for making a group of radio stations feel confident that we were representing them to our fullest potential from the all-amazing and distracting New York City. These stations were in every corner of America and would send in their national sales manager to update us on what was going on in their market, what was new on the station, and basically pump us up so we would be motivated to sell the hell out of their national advertising inventory space. Ayesha and I were naturals at sales. We started from the bottom but we quickly figured out the rules of the game. If there was a perfect friend to have at work, Ayesha was it. We encouraged each other when business was hard and when we were in tight positions with a station, a buyer, or with one of our bosses. We helped each other get our work done or stay under the radar when one of us needed additional personal time out of the office to nurse semi-depression from being so poor, hurt feelings from an argument with one of our boyfriends, or a major hangover from a night of antics only we could get ourselves into.

To personalize this a little more, my name is Farissa. I was born and raised in New York until I was fifteen years old—in the Bronx, to be more specific. I had a normal childhood—or what I thought was normal at the time. I went to school, played handball in the park with my friends, went to church with my family, and was invited to sleepovers at all the cool girls' houses.

I have a number of brothers and sisters. My dad has been married now five times. I have two older brothers from his first marriage, Anthony and Austin, who I don't have a relationship with. The last time I saw them I was around eight years old and they lived somewhere in Philadelphia. I have an older sister, Janelle, from my dad's second marriage, who until recently still lived in New York. Then there is Dad's third marriage. I am the oldest from this group, followed by my younger brother Seth. The youngest of the group is my little sister, Reaiah, who is twelve years younger than me. Since starting and finishing this book, my dad has been married two more times and the jury is still out on what will happen to the fifth one.

I know you are thinking it, so I will just say it for you—my dad is a hot mess! Yes, he has certainly gotten around. Trust me, this makes for an interesting childhood. Growing up with a father who had been married twice before meeting my mother and had moved to the States from the island of Dominica at the age of seventeen, allowed for family situations and arguments that were most likely not typical for every child in America. Both of these marriages ended on a bad note. The first one ended because my father was convinced that his second son was not his after his wife Berl gave birth. As the story goes, he constantly accused her of stepping out on him and trying to pass Austin off as his. As Austin grew older, he became very aware of this constant conversation and it started to directly affect his relationship with our father. After a few more years, I am guessing the pressure got way too much for everyone involved and it was probably my dad who decided it was time for him to move on.

His second marriage to Myrtle, my sister's mother, was much more short-lived. I am not even quite sure how they met, but she was almost ten years older than him. They dated quickly, got married quickly, got pregnant quickly, and were divorced before Janelle was two years old. Myrtle and my dad's stepmother had become very close during this short marriage due to the fact that they were of the same island mindset and that Myrtle had given my grandmother a beautiful granddaughter to be proud of. So when my father and Myrtle got divorced, my grandmother insisted that Myrtle and Janelle move in with her. That living arrangement outlived Janelle going away to college, the growth of my family, and ultimately the marriage between my mother and father. It stayed in place until my grandmother's passing in 2001.

Soon thereafter, my parents met. My mom was in nursing school taking the train between Harlem and downtown everyday and my dad was selling tokens, back when you needed a token to get through the turnstile in order to get on the platform. I am not sure how many times he sold her tokens before he decided to ask her out, but he did and after a year or so they were planning a wedding. Besides my dad's tanned, island-man good looks and muscular physique, I am not quite sure what my mom saw in a twice-divorced, father of three kids under the age of twelve, immigrant to the United States.

Looking back now, I laugh at some of the family situations that helped shape who I am today. I vividly remember a time we were at my grandmother's house. I was about the age when you are excited that the need to wear a bra outweighs your desire to wear a bra. So what is that, like ten? (Or for some, never). So, my brother was six. It was a regular occurrence that Myrtle would bring out large garbage bags of clothes that were way too small for Janelle and give them to my mom for me to try on and take whatever I liked home with us. This time was no different. We were all in the dining room, with the television probably on, eyeballing each item of clothing my mom took out of the bag. As she held up items, I would say yes or no to them. The 'yes' items would get re-folded by my mom and put in a pile for her to store in her mom bag, and the 'no' items would be put in another pile to be returned from where they came. After about fifteen minutes of this, we came to a very unique item—a bra. Even though my sister is five years older than me and I looked up to her in every way a little sister could look up to a big sister, we have always had very different bodies. We are both tall and slim, but my body has always come with curves and boobs. Janelle's came with fewer curves and significantly less boob.

Upon taking the bra out of the bag, my mom immediately checked the inside tag for the size. After a moment of reflection she said out loud to no particular person, "This is too small."

Almost without hesitation Myrtle responded, "What do you mean it's too small? Farissa is younger then Janelle. It can't be too small."

Very logically my mom responded, "Well, Farissa's breasts are already bigger than this, she wears a 32B." The silence that followed was deafening and uncomfortable for many more reasons than that my breasts were the topic of conversation, but eventually, we all moved on.

Ayesha was born in Pakistan and moved with her family to Texas when she was two years old. It was around 1983 and not too dissimilar to the current day situation in Pakistan. It was a hard place to be. Living conditions were less than ideal with the quality and access to clean water and shelter. There were daily bombs and explosions, and social freedoms of any kind were not extended to the people of this country. The decision to relocate was one her parents made in order to give Ayesha and her brother a chance at a better life. My friend comes from a very traditional Pakistani family, made up of herself and her younger brother, who is just a year or so younger than she is, and of course, her mom and dad. She also had a very normal upbringing. She played with her friends, watched MTV, and also went to the sleepovers at the cool girls' houses in Dallas. Ayesha liked to describe herself as a princess. And if a princess is someone who knows what she likes, how she likes it, and when she likes it, then she is. Don't get me wrong, I know Ayesha could come across mean and spoiled to some, but for those that got that impression, it meant they really didn't get her.

This story is about friendship, growth, and experiences. It's filled with real stories that helped make me who I am today and some that were way too funny to let go of. The great part is that while we were living them, we knew we were going to want to remember those moments forever. This story is a mixture of the laughs and the tears that have allowed us to grow as individuals, friends, and ultimately as adults.

Chapter 1

Welcome Back

I was riding in the car with Marcus, my boyfriend at the time, in Richmond, Virginia, on the way back from his younger cousin's high school graduation. It was the summer of 2005. Marcus and I had been dating at this point for seven years. We met in high school at the beginning of our senior year, which was my fourth year living in Virginia.

Looking back now, we were such an ABC Family movie. I was the new girl to the neighborhood who had moved from big, bad New York City and he was the southern-raised star athlete. I did not know one person at all my age and literally felt like I had been thrown into the deep end of the social pool when my parents relocated to Richmond in 1996—I was fifteen. It did take about two years for me to figure out where I was going to fit in this new place. I remember walking to school on the first day and wondering where the sidewalks were, where everyone else was and how they were getting to school.

As a city kid, you walk to school or take public transportation. Only the lame kids rode the yellow school bus. But in the new social construct I was now a part of, the exact opposite was true. I quickly made a small group of girlfriends and crushed on random guys I met through family connections and school. But it wasn't until I ended up in a class with Marcus White in twelfth grade that I really felt like I had found a really comfortable place.

The first thing I saw in him was his humor. He was so funny. He made me laugh, he made his friends laugh, and he even made the teachers laugh. Then I saw that he was good-looking. He was over six feet, had a body that displayed the skills he had on the football and track fields as well as the basketball court, and had a smile that automatically made you smile whether you were aware you were doing it or not. But everyone saw that, so in all honesty, it wasn't that important to me. The more I got to know him, the more I liked him and, ironically, the more I stayed away.

At the time, my girlfriend LaToya had a crush on him. She had never had a real conversation with him or even made a ripple on his radar, but that did not change the fact that he made her stomach drop whenever he walked by us. Considering the fact that I had not known anyone when I started high school and as a freshman and sophomore you have to be invited by an upperclassman to prom, I had not been to any dances my first two years of high school. I did go to my junior prom with a date that was quickly removed from my life shortly thereafter due to his lack of kissing skills.

So, come senior year, I really wanted to make sure I "did it right." The homecoming dance was right around the corner. LaToya and I were trying to decide if we were going to go. Neither one of us had dates, but that was not an issue because we had each other. A couple weeks before the dance, a friend from homeroom, Chris Drinkwater, who was also a friend of Marcus's, approached me at my locker as LaToya and I were getting our books.

"There is a rumor that Marcus is going to ask you to homecoming," he said to me with a smile on his face.

"What do you mean, a rumor?" I asked.

"He might ask you," he said quickly. I was confused and knew that I had to get to the bottom of this as there was less than two weeks to the dance and I was not prepared if I was about to be asked. So I dug a little deeper.

"Is he thinking about asking me and wondering what I would say?" I asked. I know, pretty bold, but time was ticking. I would need to find a dress, get my nails done, and get my hair done, and I was sure that all the good dresses had been picked through at the mall that late in the game.

"Well if he was going to ask you, he would need your phone number," Chris said while handing me a piece of paper and a pen. Okay, it was clear what was happening. I looked at LaToya and she was in a state of shock. I took the pen and paper and wrote my house number—because it was 1999 and only businessmen, rich people, and drug dealers had cell phones—and gave it to Chris. He took it and put it in his pocket. Before he walked away he said, "He will call you this weekend."

Before LaToya could get a word out, I asked her, "If he asks me to homecoming, would you mind if I said yes and go?" I fully intended to say yes if he called me, but in the girl code, you at least have to ask. Her face looked like she had tasted a new complicated food.

"I don't mind if you say yes, but that won't change the way I feel about him." She answered with an inflection that made it clear that only part of that was true.

Either way, I didn't care because I was more interested in the fact that I might be going to homecoming with the possible homecoming king at my first and last homecoming dance.

That weekend came and on Saturday night, the phone rang. My dad answered and I listened to see if it was for me.

"Hello?" my dad said with his cool Caribbean accent. Normally at this point, if the phone were for me, my dad would be annoyed with the etiquette of the person on the other end of the line and would interrupt them and just ask, "Would you like to speak to her?" This time, all he said was, "Yes, she is. Hold on."

I took the phone out of his hands, covered the bottom with my hand and whispered, "Who is it?"

He said, "Marcus?"

I probably smiled in a weird way that matched the feeling that instantaneously hit my stomach, turned around, and slowly walked away. I walked to the steps leading upstairs and stopped on the fourth step. It was the only place in the house that gave the illusion of privacy since I shared a room with my little sister and I could see a family member in every other room of the house.

Once I felt settled enough to use my mouth to utter words, I said, "Hello?" As soon as he started talking, I could hear a smile in his voice. He was nervous, but seemed cooler than me.

"Hey! What are you doing?" he asked.

"Nothing. Just watching TV," I answered. The real answer was that I was literally waiting for him to call me.

"Yeah, me too," he said, kind of slower than how he started the conversation. I really didn't know what else to say from here, so I just sat and waited for him to say something else.

It took awhile, but after what felt like five minutes he found his words. "So…I was calling…to ask you…if you would go to the dance with me…" he squeezed out.

I was smiling from ear to ear now. Feeling in control and not wanting to give it up too quickly, I tried to think of a witty response, but all I could think to say was, "Yes."

A cloud of weird seemed to immediately lift after that. It was almost like we had been friends forever and missed each other.

"I'm glad you didn't wait any longer to ask me. I have a lot to do now to get ready for the dance," I said as we chatted.

"What do you mean?" he asked.

"Um, I have to find a dress, make a hair appointment, get my nails done, and I only have a week," I said. The conversation went on like this for about forty-five minutes until we decided it was time to hang up.

Monday came and the whole week was like hanging out with my new bestie. We joked, he introduced me to all of his friends, and I instantly found myself part of a new crew—the popular kids—and it felt nice. The weird part was that I didn't have butterflies. I didn't daydream about kissing him. I didn't think about what it would be like to be his girlfriend. I didn't think about any of these things until that Saturday evening when I was in my upstairs bathroom putting the final touches on my hair and heard a car pull up in front of the house.

My dad was outside cutting grass and my little sister was playing with her Skipper Jump on the front lawn. I saw Marcus get out of the car. He had a fresh haircut and was wearing a tan suit with a blue shirt and a multi-colored tie. I watched from the window as he walked up to my dad, shook his hand and greeted him. My throat closed and made it impossible for me to swallow. My stomach turned upside down and I felt like I needed to sit down. There they were—the butterflies. In that moment, I know I fell in love with Marcus.

Just then my little sister, who was almost four, came running back into the house and slammed the kitchen door behind her.

"Farissa, he's here, he's here," she said in the cutest voice I will never forget.

"Yes, Reaiah. I know. I saw him out of the window in the bathroom. Do me a favor—stop yelling before he comes in, okay?"

I wanted as close to perfection as I could get during my descent down the stairs. A second later, I heard the door open again and Marcus walked in.

"Hello?" Marcus said loudly as he didn't see anyone in the house.

"She's over here," Reaiah said, not as loudly this time. Marcus walked to the bottom of the steps and looked up. He smiled and I said hello. In order to not make it too awkward, I hurried down the stairs and we hugged.

"You look nice," he said to me.

"Thanks, so do you," I said without being able to make eye contact. "Shall we go?"

From my house we went to dinner with a group and I wasn't able to eat more than three bites, I was so nervous. When we walked into the dance, I felt like I was with a famous person. Everyone knew him and also liked him. It was magnetic. Marcus won homecoming king, we danced the night away, and we kissed and kissed and kissed the following week away until we decided to date. That was our beginning.

As Marcus and I continued our car ride that summer in 2005 after attending his cousin's high school graduation, we were on the way back to his mom's house for a cookout and celebration. It was one of those days that, when looking back at it, I know changed the entire course of my life.

My cell phone rang and it was my dad.

"Farissa, I got a message on the answering machine today for you. I could not make it out, but they left a number for you to call them back. Take it down."

Ten minutes later, I was on my cell phone with great anticipation wondering who was going to be on the other line.

"Hello?" the voice on the other line said. I tried to see if I recognized it, but no one came to mind.

"Hi. Did someone call Farissa?" I asked.

"Hi, it's Lisa!" she responded with a smile in her tone. In an instant, I knew exactly to whom I was talking. Lisa Guzman was my best friend growing up in New York. When my family moved to Richmond we had tried to keep in touch. We spoke on the phone all of the time in the beginning. We wrote letters constantly and she even came out and spent a week with us during one of the summers I was in high school. But it had been a while since I had even thought of her, let alone spoken to her. Five years had gone by since our last conversation. This was so random!

"So how are things with you?" she asked as the conversation continued. I told her that I was still dating the same guy I had been the last time we spoke and things were good. We were not planning a wedding or anything, but we might buy a house soon.

"So, what about you?" I asked, really not expecting to hear anything too exciting.

"I am engaged! And the wedding is next weekend. Do you think you can make it? I would love to see you after all these years and have you meet my husband," was her full response. It took me a moment to let all of that sink in. It was a ton of new information. Not only had I just reconnected with one of the first friends I can ever remember making in life, but she was engaged and the wedding was around the corner. These are the kind of conversations that actually make life interesting! How could I not see this through? I told her that I would do some research and see if there were any flights I could afford to New York at this late notice and let her know.

After I hung up the phone, I looked at Marcus, who was driving, to get his reaction to the half conversation he had just heard.

"That was my friend Lisa. She is getting married next weekend and wants to know if we can make it to the wedding," I summed up for him.

"Where is the wedding?" he asked, completely unfazed by the enormity of the last fifteen minutes.

"It's somewhere in New York. She still lives in the Bronx, so I am sure it will be somewhere up there," I said. The longer we talked, the more it became clear that Marcus was not interested in going to New York.

"How much are flights to New York?" he asked.

"I am sure it will be at least a couple hundred dollars for both of us," I answered.

"I don't have that kind of money right now," he snapped back.

"Well we can drive up together and stay with my sister like we did last time we went. Then all we have to pay for is gas and tolls," I said, thinking I was solving the problem. But he was not having it.

"I just don't feel like going," he said, ending the conversation.

That Monday, I decided I was going to New York by myself and I would take my sister as my date to the wedding. We always had a great time together. Even though we never got to experience what it was like growing up in the same house, as young adults we started hanging out in New York City together whenever we could, and knew how to shut shit down, if you know what I mean.

Because there were no flights that I could afford at that late notice, I decided I was going to take my car and hit the highway. I called my sister and told her that I was staying with her this weekend and she was all about it. It was the end of June and hot as hell. I left my job as early as I could that Friday without being missed and hit the road with a bunch of CDs, a soda, and a fresh pack of cigarettes.

The drive was faster than I expected. I had made this trip tons of times as a child in the back seat with my father driving and my mother yelling that she had to go to the bathroom AGAIN. I had plenty of time—seven hours to be exact—to think. I sang all of my favorite songs out loud, scanned the dial for the local radio stations as I made it to different cities and contemplated life and its meaning and what I really wanted to do with my life. Crossing the George Washington Bridge from New Jersey into New York was always special and this time did not disappoint. As I drove across, I imagined being there and never having to leave, wearing tailored suits and running for cabs. All of a sudden, it felt like something I had to do and no longer a daydream. I called my mom.

"I think I want to move back to New York," I told her.

"Are you crazy?" she asked me very seriously. "You would do that to me? You would need a job." She went on as if she was just thinking about things to say to change my mind. None of it fazed me.

"I know. I would not move up here without a job. I will find one and then move," I replied.

"You wouldn't just leave Marcus would you?" she asked in a different tone that suggested she had figured out I was serious.

"No, he would come with me," I replied confidently.

After that conversation, I could not stop thinking about it, how amazing it would be to live this adventure and where it would all take me. The wheels in my head started spinning and would not stop. That was the beginning of my real life.

At the same time in Dallas, Ayesha was starting a new job at a company called Interep. This position was as an account executive and national sales rep. She would now be responsible for selling advertising for a group of stations all owned by one company scattered all around the United States. She would have to do this by building relationships with media buyers at agencies in Dallas who also bought advertising nationally. She had no idea what she was doing. She later confessed to me that all she did was sit in the office and watch people do their job for a while until she picked it up.

Interep normally does not hire people from outside the company and make them account executives right away. They want them to start out as assistants, but she told them she wasn't doing that. There was no way she was going to take a pay cut from one job to the next. She needed her money so she could afford whatever she wanted. You know, getting her nails done, buying plane tickets to New York every other weekend to see her new "friend," all while looking fly in the process.

She was there for a month in that position when one day her manager came to her with some news. "The company has this training program that we do once a year where account executives who get hired into the company go through a thirteen-week program," she started. "They learn the ins and outs of radio and how to be a great seller. And we want you to do it," she said.

So far it all sounded fine. It was a move in the right direction and would make her better at a job that she was just starting to grasp. "And it's in New York," her boss added. "The company will pay for you to go out there for thirteen weeks and live. There is a house that all the people in training live in rent-free during the program. How does all of this sound to you?" she finally asked.

It all seemed too good to be true. All Ayesha could focus on was the last part of that speech which sounded to her like her boss had said *Sex & The City*, almost without hesitation Ayesha had a response. "That sounds great!" she said still stung with happiness. That was enough for her boss to continue. "We will have this job waiting for you here once you are done with the program, which means we will sponsor you," she explained.

Not all of the people who got into the program, if already with the company, were promised a job at the end of it. The company had the right to send the non-sponsored reps to any Interep office that needed them at the time. But for Ayesha, the whole thing was set up. She would go to New York the first weekend of October, stay for thirteen weeks, train, come back to Dallas when it was over and sell her little heart out. That was Ayesha's beginning.

Chapter 2

How Things Change: Rewind

"Oh, by the way, if you are coming up here this weekend, bring a bathing suit. I have a pool party to go to on Saturday that you are coming to. What day is the wedding you have to go to?"

My sister, Janelle, sounded excited that I was going to New York that weekend. "The wedding is on Sunday," I responded, "but that is all I know. I told Lisa I would call her when I got up there so I could get the rest of the details. I have no idea where it is or what time it even starts. I'm going to leave work on Friday at three p.m. so I can get to New York at nine or ten, enough time so we can go out!" I told her.

It had been a while since I had been back to New York, and my childhood best friend's wedding was a perfect excuse to get back.

"Okay, see you then. Love ya," Janelle said in her usual, quirky way.

That Friday night the traffic was decent toward the beginning of the trip. I cruised through Virginia then hit D.C. and then was stuck for hours. Once that traffic cleared up, I sailed through Maryland and Delaware, and New Jersey was no problem. I got to my sister's house around ten p.m. and had no time to relax. Immediately, it was time for me to put on my going out clothes, per her orders, for a night out on the town.

My sister had told a few of her friends that I was coming into town for the weekend and that they should meet us Friday night. They had started their night already and it was up to us to find them. My sister put in a few calls to figure out where the crew was and within minutes, we were in a cab headed uptown to a lounge that happened to be owned by one of my sister's friends from grade school. We met up with a group of guys and for hours enjoyed the attention of being the only women in the group. We ate and drank and got louder as the night went on.

As usual on my trips to New York, the night ended many vodka cranberries later at three in the morning and with me knocked out on my sister's bed. Hours later, our eyes opened and it was noon. The pool party was supposed to start at three, but we couldn't move.

"I don't even know if I have a clean bathing suit that I'd like to wear to this thing today," Janelle said as she looked for anything that resembled a clean bathing suit in her room. It looked like a hurricane had gone through it and all that was left was a mountain of t-shirts and clothes from Banana Republic and Ann Taylor.

"I'm sure you have one somewhere," I said optimistically, trying to take time off the search. She finally found a few mix-matched bathing suit pieces and spent the next half hour demanding the truth from me about how she looked in each bathing suit she could find. She thought she was getting fat. She informed me that they call it the Wall Street tummy or something. Basically, women who are fit and beautiful get jobs on Wall Street and work for a couple years and all of a sudden find a little extra something in the midsection that wasn't there before, due to the late hours, horrible eating habits, and the six figures that they are making each year.

"Do you mind if we pick up one of my friends on the way to the party?" she asked, offering up a good change of topic. "He was supposed to come out with us last night but never made it. He lives in Brooklyn," she finished.

"No problem," I said. The car I had driven up in was actually Marcus's and was a small, two-door hatchback. It wasn't going to be that glamorous, but we would get there. Janelle called her friend right away to make sure he was still coming, to let him know what the plans were, and to give him shit for not showing up last night. She ended the conversation by getting directions to his place, and told him what time we would be there. From their conversation and the references made by the group last night, I was confused as to what his name was as he had been called two different names consistently.

"Is his name James or Larry?" I asked. "'Cause you called him both on the phone just now," I said, finally interested enough to get to the bottom of it.

"His name is Larry, but his friends call him James—just so you don't get confused today," she answered. It made no sense to me why that would be the case, but my interest level truly did stop there for the moment. I would find out later that his middle name was James and eventually start to feel part of the lucky few that called him by that name instinctually.

An hour later we were in the car headed over the Brooklyn Bridge to the Brooklyn side to pick up Larry. I was wearing a black two-piece bikini that was outlined with white, a white tank top, and a peach and white floral maxi skirt with strappy sandals. Of course we got lost because my sister was driving and she did not write down the directions Larry had given her earlier on the phone. We finally got there and waited on the corner of Willow and Pierpont because we knew we were close.

After a couple of minutes, there was a nicely built light-skinned guy walking toward the car. He had on a pair of khaki shorts that were half an inch too short for my taste, and a patterned shirt he wore unbuttoned over a faded green t-shirt. My first thought of him was that he was the best-looking geek I had ever seen, but he could not dress for shit.

"Oh man, I forgot my bathing suit," were the first words out of his mouth as he approached the car. "I don't feel like going back upstairs. I'll just buy one on the way," he said to my sister. I hoped she would talk him out of that. With the long drive upstate we already had ahead of us, the last thing I wanted to think about was finding a place to buy a bathing suit.

"Stop being so lazy. Just go back upstairs and get your bathing suit. We'll wait for you," she said to my delight. And with that, he turned around and walked away again to get his bathing suit. Once he was far enough out of sight for me to feel comfortable to talk about him, I did.

"Did he forget where we were going?" I asked, annoyed. My sister had no comment and just giggled. He finally came back downstairs, and I got out of the car for the first time since we had been there in order to introduce myself and give him room to get into the back seat.

"Hi, I'm Farissa," I said.

"Hi—wow! I'm surrounded by Amazon women," he said to me without even a moment of space between my introduction and his one-liner. I had no response to that. I gave him a pity smile with no teeth and proceeded to bend my seat forward so he could climb in the back. My sister and I got into the car and got ready for the hour-long ride in front of us.

For the next two hours, because of course we got lost, we drowned in easy, enjoyable conversation. We got hungry and went through the McDonald's drive-through. We took turns telling our current relationship stories. I talked about my plans to buy a house with Marcus, Janelle confessed how crazy her relationship with her boyfriend was and how she had only been to his house five times in the past six years.

Larry showed me a picture of his three kids on his cell phone. We smoked tons of cigarettes between the three of us and by the end of our journey, I felt like that conversation was really the reason I woke up that day, not the pool party. I was confused about whether or not I should be buying a house with Marcus and my secret desire to move back to New York was heightened by a million. The most interesting part of it all was that the geek that got into the back seat of my boyfriend's car in Brooklyn was now all of a sudden the most charming, stimulating man I had ever met. What the hell!?

When we finally got there, the rest of the afternoon was full of great food, Janelle's old friends, the pool, the sun, a farm full of animals, and one-on-one moments with Larry. We snuck away from the group, to what I'm sure looked like to them, share a smoke, but for us, even though we never called it this, it was our first chance to feel what it felt like to be alone with each other.

We walked along the gate where the farm animals were being held and Larry talked about everything he knew about each animal: the goats, the llamas, the chickens, and the roosters. It was like hanging out with an encyclopedia. We got to know each other and it never felt weird. It was as natural as picking up the phone and calling a friend. As we headed back to the main house, we could see that everyone was trying to decide what we should all do next.

When Larry and I walked into the house we ended our personal conversation and became part of the group again.

"I can't find my phone," Larry said to me as we entered the house. "Do you mind if I use yours to call it?" he asked.

"Sure, no problem," I said as I handed him my phone. I watched him punch in his phone number and waited to hear the ringing of his phone. In a moment's time, we heard the chime of what Larry confirmed to be his ringer coming from under a pile of towels and clothes brought in from the poolside. Larry walked over to it and picked up his phone to dismiss the call. Without hesitation he walked back over to me and handed me my phone back.

"Thank you," he said.

"You're welcome."

And just like that, we had each other's digits.

Around the time the sun went down, the group decided we would all meet up in the city that night and go out. Around eleven p.m., we were all showered and changed and ready to get into whatever the night had to offer. Since I was staying at my sister's house and Larry had to come into the city from Brooklyn, we decided he should meet us at her place so we could meet up with everyone together. Larry had also invited a friend of his from his hometown of Chicago, who was also living in New York now.

He described her as "just a friend." My sister and I were both curious, so she pressed him.

"So you guys have never slept together?" she asked.

"No. We're just friends," he replied calmly.

"But that doesn't mean you don't want to," she said, not really asking a question.

"I don't know what that means," Larry said. "I'm not trying to sleep with her," he added, "if that is what you are trying to say."

"I guess the real question should be then, is she trying to sleep with you?" I chimed in right as Janelle's doorbell rang.

"I guess we will find out," she said as she opened the door. Her name was Stephanie. She was shorter than both me and my sister, so she did not qualify for the Amazon Women club. She was very pretty and slender. She had tanned light skin and shoulder-length hair. You could tell she was slightly older and more conservative than both my sister and I. We later learned that she was a pharmaceutical sales rep, had a child, and was single. When she walked in, she gave Larry a nice long, intimate hug, which gave my sister and I plenty of time to side-eye each other and smirk. We all had a drink while getting to know each other a little better and then headed downstairs to catch a cab.

We were going to Marquee. It was one of the hot spots at the time, frequented by people like Paris Hilton and Lindsay Lohan. It was in the Meatpacking District so it was fairly close to my sister's apartment in Tribeca. We were the first part of the group to arrive, so we posted up on the sidewalk beside the people waiting to get in. We didn't join the ridiculous line because Janelle and Larry's co-worker was going to be able to get us in without waiting. As the four of us waited outside and people watched, Stephanie started to not look so well. She was leaning back on a parked car taking deep breaths.

"Are you okay?" I asked her.

"I'm not sure," she said, trying to catch her breath.

At that point, my sister and Larry also started to notice something was wrong and they gathered around. I was standing directly to Stephanie's right, Larry was standing directly in front of her, and my sister was to my right slightly. In that next moment, Stephanie pulled off either one of the craziest female tricks around or just got lucky. She started to look like her balance was leaving her and a second later, she was falling into Larry's arms, head first into his chest. As soon as her head hit his chest, she regained her composure and stood up weakly.

"I think I need to go home," she said. "I am not feeling too well. I am sorry guys."

I was too much in shock to respond. Larry was holding her in a way that would prevent her from falling again.

"Let me get a cab for you," Larry said as he helped her to the corner.

"Thanks," she said, almost making me feel bad for her. Until she asked this:

"Will you ride home with me to make sure I make it home safely?"

That was the strongest game I had ever seen a woman play. Larry, being a gentleman, said he would and then told us he would be back. As much as I wanted to believe him, I thought there was no way he was going to make it back to the club, and even if he did, there was no way he'd make it in time to get in with the group. It was over. She won and was going to be able to spend the evening with him and I probably would never see him again. The thought never occurred to me that it really was none of my business. Janelle and I watched Larry and Stephanie get in a cab and ride away in silence. We didn't have to say anything to each other about what just happened, we were thinking the same thing.

As we continued to wait outside for Janelle's friends, Carmello Anthony, the famous NBA player and Lala, a famous television personality, who were engaged at the time, pulled up and went into the club. A few minutes later, the rest of our group pulled up in two separate cabs and piled out. We caught them up on why Larry was missing. They all got a good laugh and Michael, my sister's friend with the hookup, proceeded to get us all into the club. About forty-five minutes had gone by and there was a half-empty bottle of vodka, an opened bottle of tequila, some orange juice, cranberry juice, and seltzer water on our table and we all were feeling the positive effects of that missing liquid. With every bass beat coming out of the speakers our spirits got higher and higher.

At the very moment I forgot about Larry and the fact that he was not there, I saw him making his way through the crowd toward us. My heartskipped a beat when our eyes locked. When the rest of the group saw him, we all screamed out his name in unison. It really was the only way to collectively express to him how happy we were he was with us and didn't fall for the trap. It was the perfect New York City night. We partied, danced, and drank until five in the morning. Larry and I danced with our bodies pressed against each other for what seemed like hours as if we were placed on this earth solely for each other's pleasure.

As the club closed and everyone piled out into the hot summer morning sun, Larry, Janelle, and I found ourselves in some restaurant wanting breakfast at six in the morning. Somehow we managed to order and wait for our food. I was so drunk the thought of putting any liquid to my lips—the ice water in front of me included—made me want to throw up. But when the food arrived, I was able to stuff my face with some over-priced shrimp tacos and then eventually forced myself to have sips of water.

At the end of the meal, Larry got up and went to the bathroom. As soon as he was out of earshot, my sister leaned into me and whispered, "Would you think badly of me if I went home with him tonight?"

She was talking about Larry. That was completely unexpected. In the almost twenty-four hours we had been hanging out, I never picked up on the fact that she might be into him. Flirting? Yes. Wanting attention? Yes. But that is how she acts with everybody. And she had just gotten out of this crazy relationship that wrecked her. This was her co-worker. If something were going to happen, shouldn't it have already happened before tonight?

This was drunk Janelle talking. But no matter, I had to say something and I had to say something fast before Larry came out of the bathroom. In that moment, I decided to go with my gut and it was telling me that I could never let that happen and that I wanted him to be mine—even if it was just once! So I gave my sister the only answer I could think of at the time.

"I wouldn't think badly of you, but is this what you want to do? Is that what he wants to do? You have to see him at work on Monday."

Then I just stared at her and watched her digest that information. I could see it was working.

Just as Larry was walking back to the table, Janelle leaned in to me and said, "You're right."

A feeling of complete relief came over me because I had successfully stopped anything from happening that I wouldn't be able to live with—yes, it was all about what I wanted, and I wanted him!

Lisa never called me back to give me the information about where her wedding was, so the three of us hung out on Sunday, too. We went to brunch and walked around Brooklyn. We went to a wine store and bought wine to sip on that evening while we sat on Larry's couch listening to music and eating take-out. It was like a perfect date, just with three people.

Monday morning came and it was time to go back to the real world. Janelle and Larry had to go to work and I had to drive back to Richmond. I drove Janelle to the office before I hit the highway so I could see Larry one more time. By now I was head over heels with a guy that I had no plans to ever see again. We called him from the car when I pulled up in front of their office building so he could come down and say goodbye. When he came down, he was in a navy blue suit with a pink and white striped shirt that worked in his favor. My sister must have felt that we needed a moment because she said goodbye to me and gave us a second to say our goodbyes privately. It was the quietest we were with each other all weekend.

As I got into my car and prepared for my six-hour drive back, he looked at me like I was the most beautiful person he had ever seen and told me that he hoped to see me again. As soon as I got outside of the city, I called him and we spoke until my phone battery died.

If I were to let Ayesha tell it, she would say that she and her boyfriend, Steve, were a one-night fling gone badly. They both happened to be in Las Vegas on the same weekend with separate groups of friends. It was one of those nights where the girls were out to turn up and the boys were out to get girls.

When Ayesha and Steve saw each other for the first time, she decided he was the one for the night. The next day she was all set to act like nothing happened, something we often have to do in situations like this, but he called her and wanted to hang out the next night, too. After the Las Vegas trip, they spoke off and on for a while and sent each other e-mails. But nothing had the chance to develop because she lived in Dallas and he lived in New York.

Months later, Steve was going to Texas for a business meeting and decided to call Ayesha to ask her how close she lived to where he would be. As fate would have it, she was right around the corner. They hung out all weekend and spoke every day after that. They took turns flying each month to see each other and the relationship grew into something more. A few months later, Ayesha got the job at Interep.

Upon my return to Richmond, I had major decisions to make. All in one weekend I had made the decision to attempt to move to the largest, scariest, most awesome city in the United States and had met a person that was making me second guess the entire future I had seen for myself just days ago. I decided to go home and test the waters of my career and my relationship.

I pulled all of my resources together to figure out how to make this dream of mine a reality. I asked around at the radio station to see if anyone had any contacts in New York and what they would do if they wanted to move to New York. I lucked out when I was out at a bar with some co-workers one day for happy hour and started chatting with one of the newer sales people at our sister station. Her name was Jackie and she had just moved back to Richmond from Chicago. She was about ten years older then me, but had a very young personality, so I felt like I could trust her to keep all of my questions to herself while still being interested enough to help me figure it all out.

"I am thinking about leaving Richmond and moving to New York. But I need a few leads on jobs out there before I can make any moves," I said to her once I felt like it would be worth my while. I finished with, "What would you do if you were me?"

After just a second she was dropping insight and knowledge. "I have a friend in New York who is also my old boss. He is always looking for good sales people and I could send him an e-mail with your resume and introduce you two," she said.

"That would be amazing," I responded. I had to stop myself from talking too loudly.

"What does he do?" I asked.

"He runs a division of a company called Interep that is responsible for selling national advertising for radio stations all across the country," she answered.

"Wow, okay. That is something I could definitely do. What other companies do that out of New York?" I asked with anticipation of finding them and setting up multiple interviews. Jackie gave me the names of a couple others and promised she would send that e-mail introduction the next day.

Being that I had not really approached the topic of moving to New York with Marcus, I decided to test the relationship waters next. That night at home, I told Marcus about my latest obsession. I told him how it hit me on the drive up and that I wanted to at least try. I basically shouted, "We should move to New York!"

I was still ignoring the fact that even though I was in love with Marcus and we had something real that could potentially last a lifetime, I had met a man a few weeks ago that I had secretly spoken to every day since leaving New York. A guy that made me feel like none of the worries about life really existed the way I thought they did. Instead of focusing on that right now, I decided to test Marcus to see if he would even entertain the idea of moving to New York together.

"So what do you think?" I asked after my speech.

"So you want to move to New York? One of the most expensive cities in the country with no job?" he asked.

"No," I started. "I want to find a job in New York, find us an apartment to live in that we can afford, and then help you find a job and think of it as an adventure."

"We can barely afford to pay our bills here and our families are here," he said.

"Yeah, but just because we move somewhere doesn't mean we have to live there forever. We can always move back when we are older and ready to have kids," I argued. But he was not having it. We had too much debt, he hadn't found his dream job (which for me was another reason to try and leave), and was not excited by the element of the unknown like I was.

"Well what if I told you I was going to try and find a job in New York whether or not you want to come with me?" I asked after deciding with myself it was my next move.

"I am not moving to New York, so do whatever you want to do," he said, testing me in his own way.

The next day, Jackie forwarded me an e-mail from her contact in New York. It read: "I would love to meet your friend. If she is anything like you, I am sure we could find a place for her. I am in the process of looking for applicants for our next Rapper program, anyway. Tell her to call me."

I read below his e-mail to see that Jackie had said some really nice things about me to Bruce. It was happening much faster than I thought it all would, and it wasn't going to be because of me that it slowed down. Just when I was deciding on when to call Bruce and how I would handle myself in that conversation, James called. We had not let a day go by since we met without having at least one phone conversation and sending multiple e-mails.

We were dating long distance from the moment I got back in my car to head back to Richmond. We talked about everything. Me moving to New York, my relationship with Marcus, his relationship with his ex-wife, his relationship with his kids, his negative outlook on relationships and marriage vs. my positive, romantic view on these exact things, and what we could potentially be doing. This time the call was a quick one. He just had a question.

"If I booked a hotel room in D.C. for a weekend, would you drive up from Richmond and meet me halfway?" he asked with grown-man intentions.

I enjoyed letting that question soak into my ears, mind, and thoughts before answering moments later.

"Yes."

"Okay. Good. That is what I'd hoped you'd say. Let me set it all up and I will e-mail you the address of the hotel and I will see you soon. I can fly down on a Friday night. Could you come up then?" he asked.

"That should be fine," I said.

"What will you tell Marcus?" he asked.

"Don't worry about that," I answered. Not wanting to muddy the sexiness of this conversation. In all reality, I had already figured it out. I would tell Marcus that I was staying with my friend in D.C. who Marcus knew about but had never met.

The next day I was fully prepared to call Bruce, Jackie's old boss and potentially my new one, in New York. It was a quick call. He asked about my experience, what I wanted out of the next step in my career, and he explained the Rapper program to me. It was a basic training program that prepared his sales team for the national playground. It would teach me what advertising agencies with multi-million dollar budgets needed from people like me to make their lives easier. The call ended with us setting a date the next month for me to interview in person for a spot in the training program. It really couldn't have gone any better.

It was now the beginning of August. I was headed to D.C. that weekend to spend it with James and I had just booked my flight (with my dad's credit card) to New York for my interviews a few weeks later. I was able to book an interview with the competitor company to Interep for the same day based on everything Jackie taught me that night in the bar.

Marcus was beside himself that I was able to make so much progress and I was through the moon. I had never been so excited about life and the possibilities of everything to come. But one thing at a time has always been my motto. I never liked getting too excited about what could happen because I have always felt that it distracts you from what you should be doing to get that amazing thing to happen. Instead I focused on the little things like a bikini wax, shaving my legs, exfoliating my face, outfit planning, underwear or no underwear—you know, the normal list of items to freak out about when planning a weekend trip with your secret lover with whom you have not had sex with...yet.

That Friday night, I made it to D.C. around eight. James's flight was supposed to land right before nine. He gave me the check-in information so I could get there, get comfortable, and then pick him up from the airport once his flight landed. Of course, his flight was delayed. So I found myself sitting in a hotel room, by myself, watching reruns , eating a slice of pizza, waiting for his flight to get in. I did anything I could to take my mind off of my nerves.

There was a definite chemistry between us, even over the phone, but who was to say we would even like each other in a different, more intimate environment? What if he wasn't as good looking as I remembered? What if we had nothing to talk about and this was the worst weekend ever? I secretly was hoping for an epic fail on all fronts so that it would make the decision that I knew was looming in front of me easier to make. I didn't want to have to break up with Marcus because I found something better. If we were going to break up, I wanted it to be because he wasn't the one for me and did not support my dreams. I wanted whatever was going to happen with James this weekend to be the worst—sex included—so I could have proof that what I had really wasn't so bad.

I finally got a text from James around nine forty-five that his plane had landed. The hotel he booked was pretty close to the airport, so I jumped in the car and headed to pick him up. I cherished the last few moments of solitude before pulling up to the curb and unlocking the door for the man I recognized in a blue-striped, button-down shirt, khaki dress pants, and brown shoes. He got in the car and kissed me on the cheek before saying anything.

"Hi. Sorry I'm late. I am beat. The flight was delayed an hour and we made up time in the air. I've been up since six this morning working so I wouldn't have to work this weekend. But I am here and very happy about it. Do I look as good as you remember?" he asked me as he lit a cigarette.

The real answer was that I didn't remember. But I said, "Yes." We talked about what to do for dinner and if we should go out. I told him I had eaten while waiting for him but we could still go somewhere so he could eat and we could have some drinks. As we dropped his bag off at the hotel, we spotted a bar not too far that had an open patio, live music, and open seats. So we walked over, got a table on the patio, and ordered a pitcher of cold beer to counter the steamy August night.

It was easy from the beginning. We told each other stories like old friends catching up at a reunion. We talked about work as if we had been dating for years. And when there was silence, there was no awkwardness. It was actually more like how it feels to take a deep breath when you sit down after a brisk walk—refreshing. The only time I got nervous was when I let my mind slip into wondering what experience could possibly await me back at the hotel. But before I could wander too far down that mental road, he was starting a new interesting conversation.

When the pitcher was empty, we decided it was time to close the tab and head back to the hotel. The ten minute trip back was made mostly in silence, for which I was glad. I needed that time to try and figure out my next steps. Do I put on my pj's in the bathroom and then climb in bed and go to sleep? Do I change in front of him so he knows that I am open to destiny figuring out what happens next? Am I really that brave? Is there talking during this changing? Do I call them PJs? This was major new territory for me and I had no idea what I was doing. By the time we pulled into the parking lot of the hotel, I still had no idea, so I decided to just not talk much and follow my gut. We walked out of the car together into the lobby of the hotel. The front desk clerk greeted me.

"Welcome back Mrs. Knox," he said.

James and I both ignored it and smiled at him as not to be rude. Once in the room, we sat on the bed and both had a real exhale to commemorate the day we had just lived.

The tension was heavy. Even though, on the surface, we were just taking our shoes off, turning on music and getting comfortable, underneath our skin, there was a chemical energy building. I was leaning into it willing to let it cover me like a blanket on a chilly night, but he was doing everything in his power to prevent himself from falling prey to it.

This was now familiar territory. All of our long distance phone conversations would get to this point: flirty and enticing but ultimately safe.

Now with nothing but a couple of inches between us, there was nothing stopping us from exploring what we came to find out.

Not wanting to be the one to initiate the game, I got up to put on my pajamas. I had decided that if he was going to pretend he didn't want to kiss me, I was going to show him what he was missing. I dimmed the lights and unzipped my overnight bag. I pulled out the clothes I was going to change into while James sat on the edge of the bed watching me in silent awe. He knew from our conversation the night before that I was contemplating not wearing anything under my clothes just to make things interesting. I turned my back to him and slid my silk cami over my head and dropped it. Before it hit the floor, James was standing in front of me with his hands on my arms, pulling me into his space. Our first kiss was exactly what a girl hopes her last first kiss would be. We kissed for a few moments before I felt his fingers on the strings of my linen pants. As those came undone and fell to the floor, my feet left the floor. He laid me on the bed with ease and never took his eyes off of me while he undressed and made his way to me. We made love.

Our weekend was amazing. We ate breakfast in bed. We made love. We went to the zoo. We made love. We ate shrimp on the pier. We made love. We went to dinner—then went to sleep.

It was everything I hoped it wouldn't be. I didn't want to have to know that the connection I felt the day I met James was real and therefore would require that I shake my life up—no matter if I ended up with James or not.

I went back to Richmond and continued the job search.

As the weeks passed, Marcus could tell there was something different about me. My weekend in D.C. had put the final piece of straw in our relationship and I was going to leave him once I figured out how.

I had secured a couple of interviews in New York over the course of a couple days and drove up again. I stayed with James and it was even more magical. It took a few more weeks before I heard back from any of the jobs. Simultaneously while trying to land a job in New York, as a backup plan, I found myself a studio apartment I was ready to sign the lease on in downtown Richmond in case I needed to stay. No matter what happened with New York—a job, no job, Larry, no Larry. I was going to break up with Marcus and tell him I was moving out. Then I got the call. I got into the training program at Interep and was officially moving to New York! Even though I knew it was the right thing to do, it was hard leaving Marcus. I knew I was breaking his heart and that I was picking myself over our relationship, but I had to try for something bigger and better in every aspect of my life or I know I would have died inside. In retrospect, I could have handled the situation (the breakup and simultaneous move) much better and still gotten to the same place. But I was young and not experienced enough in relationships of any kind to know better. Marcus and I were friends and are not anymore—lesson learned.

It was now the last week in September. I left Richmond on a Friday morning. My dad drove me up to New York with as many of my clothes as I could fit in the car and my cat, Buddy Snuggles. He dropped me off at the house in Yonkers that my company rented for the trainees to stay in during the twelve week session. It was almost like going back to college for a few weeks to learn advertising sales—boot camp style. I unpacked my stuff and picked my room before any of my housemates showed up and then went right into the city to hang out for the whole weekend before I had to be in a classroom at seven-thirty that Monday morning. After a calm weekend of catching up with my sister and some friends, my sister drove me back to Yonkers on Sunday night and I officially met my roommates.

"Hi, I'm Tiffany," announced a tall, slim, White girl with long blond hair. My first impression was that she was a cheerleader or something. "Hi, I'm Farissa, nice to meet you. Where are you from?" I asked, as her accent had thrown me off.

"Detroit," she answered. "I worked as an assistant for Interep in the Detroit office. What office did you come from?" she asked me.

"I didn't already work for Interep," I answered. "I live in Richmond and worked for a radio station there and sold for them locally. I am from New York originally and am ready to move back. I hope after training I am able to just stay here."

At that moment, an equally tall, but not as slim Black girl came out of one of the bedrooms.

"Hi, I'm Kali," she introduced.

"Hi. Farissa. And where are you from?" I asked her.

"I just graduated from Howard. I am from New York, too, but my mom moved to Detroit when she and my dad divorced.

And then I got into Howard and just graduated. Interep came to my school for a career day and that's how I got here," she explained.

First impressions: very young and wet behind the ears.

And I could say that from the perspective of my ripe old age of twenty-four. The rest of the night we talked about ourselves some more and the other roommate. Apparently, she knew some people who lived in Queens and was visiting with them that night. I would meet her in the morning.

After we had all taken showers the next morning, I had a brief encounter with Sandra. She was the fourth roommate. We had no time to be cordial due to the train schedule. We ran to catch ours into the city at six twenty-five a.m. and an hour later, we were into our first day of training. We were situated in a conference room at a round table and I took survey of the room. There was Jason, the Jewish boy from Queens who was an assistant for Interep's New York office. He was blond and talked like a typical New Yorker, but with a flair that would fit right in California somewhere.

Eric, the white boy from Brooklyn who was also an assistant in the New York office was quiet and laid back. He seemed excited and nervous at the same time. Gordan, the black guy from the Chicago office was all smiles. He was also excited and nervous. I automatically thought I would have no problem getting along with him. And then there was Judd. He was a white boy from Queens who you could tell had a lot to say. He was an assistant in the New York office, as well. As the introductions continued, I learned that my fourth roommate, Sandra, was from Los Angeles and worked as an assistant for the office there. In addition to my other roommates, there was one more girl to introduce herself. It was Ayesha.

The next few hours were filled with more introductions of ourselves, our instructor, Bruce, and what we were to expect from this class. We would be required to memorize every piece of information that he put in front of us. This included all of the information we just learned about each other, down to how many sisters and brothers Sandra had and what would be Tiffany's dream job—questions that I can still answer today.

Needless to say, at the end of the twelve weeks, we all knew each other very well. We all did almost everything together, especially those of us who lived in the same house. Gordan got the apartment next door to us girls all to himself. Ayesha was supposed to be his roommate, but stayed in the city the entire time. Come to think of it, Ayesha was supposed to do a lot of things that she didn't.

She did stay over at the girls' apartment one night for a slumber party that led to a group brunch at Bruce's house the next day.

By now we were halfway through our training and it was nearing the end of November.

Bruce invited us all to a breakfast event, which explained the benefits of the new technology Terrestrial Radio was going to use to stay up-to-date with all the growing competition. It was HD radio. The instructions from Bruce were that we had to meet in our conference room at seven-thirty a.m. as usual and then all walk as a group to this breakfast at the MetLife building in Midtown. At seven forty-five we all realized that Ayesha was nowhere to be found. Because Ayesha had been late before, we waited a while before it became a big deal. Someone made a joke, "How funny would it be if Ayesha was still sleeping?" Another five minutes passed and the situation became real.

"Maybe one of us should call her," suggested Sandra.

She picked up her phone and we all got quiet to hear the conversation.

"It's ringing," she said.

"Hey, where are you?" We could hear her ask. That was then quickly followed up by her next question.

"Did you just wake up? We have that breakfast this morning," she reminded Ayesha. It became clear that the exact situation we had all joked about was really happening.

Ten minutes later, we had all worked out a plan for when Bruce showed up and wanted to know where Ayesha was. We would say that she thought we were all supposed to meet at the breakfast and she was going to meet us there. It worked, but he was not happy. Across town, Ayesha was running around Steve's apartment yelling, looking for clothes, and freaking out! She threw on something to wear from the floor, grabbed socks and shoes, and ran out the door—morning breath and all. Later I found out she actually ran down New York sidewalks with no shoes or socks on in the middle of November looking for a cab.

When we all showed up at the breakfast, Ayesha was still not there. Our story was starting to unravel. Bruce was so mad that he threatened if any of us got a call on our cell phones from Ayesha and reminded her where the breakfast was, we would get kicked out of the program! With two minutes to go before the breakfast started, she came walking in.

It was now December. The class would be over in three weeks and no one knew where they were going to be living after it was over. At this point, Bruce had called all of us into his office individually to tell us about openings around the country that he thought we would be good for. I was either going to Philadelphia, Chicago, or staying in New York. I made it my goal to stay in New York. There was nothing that anyone could say that would change my mind. My problem was that all of the openings in New York were allocated to the assistants that they had sponsored, Jason and Eric. I felt my dream slipping away from me but kept a positive mindset that it would all work out.

That is when Frank Howard, a director of sales in the New York office, wanted to speak with me. At first it was just in an attempt to get to know me. So I made sure he knew I was from New York and would fit right in here. I also made sure he knew how much of a hard worker I was and how dedicated to success I was. A few conversations later, we talked about the opening he had and the type of person he wanted to fill it. He needed someone who could cover some agencies out of the New York office to travel to Philadelphia to call on agencies in that area and call on some of the larger agencies in RICHMOND. Agencies I could only dream of calling on when I lived and worked in Richmond, like The Martin Agency, were now being given to me to work with as the new kid on the block. This was perfect for me. I would get to live and stay in New York, see where this relationship with James could go, and regularly fly back to Richmond for work and see my family. It was a dream come true.

The day of the office Christmas party, it was official. I had my position in the New York office that I would start in two weeks. It was time to start looking for an apartment! Everything had worked out the way

I always saw it working in my head. It almost made me feel like I had manifested it into reality.

Unfortunately, everything did not work out as smoothly for Ayesha. Toward the end of the program, the job that the Dallas office had promised would be waiting for her was instead given to a senior account executive who decided she wanted to move back to Dallas from Los Angeles.

After many conversations and doubts, Ayesha was left with two options: become a non-sponsored rep and get placed anywhere around the country like the rest of us, or just finish the program and have Bruce help her find a job at a different company if she decided she wanted to stay in New York.

Ayesha did not want to take the chance of being sent anywhere in the country. She had fallen in love with her boyfriend and the thought of going back to Dallas was not at all appealing. In true Ayesha form, she decided to seize the day and take the no job option. After all, how hard could it be to find a job in advertising in New York? Two months later, with a Rapper program diploma and still no job, Ayesha got a phone call from Bruce. He wanted to let her know there was an opening in his department that he wanted her to interview for. The network department was growing and taking on additional roles within the company and in order to accomade all of this growth, he needed a good sales person and, of course, thought of her first...and the rest is history!

Jason stayed in New York to work for the CBS group; Eric stayed in New York to work for the D&R group; Tiffany (originally from Detroit) went to Los Angeles to work for the ABC group; Sandra went back to Los Angeles to work for the CBS group; Gordan went to Los Angeles to work for the McGavern group; Judd went to San Francisco to work for the D&R group; I stayed in New York to work for the Susquehanna group; and Ayesha took a little while longer than the others, but eventually was placed in Bruce's network department in New York. And this is when Ayesha and I really got to know each other.

Why are women such long-term planners? We can't help it. It's in our blood, in our nature. When we start dating someone new, we immediately start thinking about where the relationship could go, what its fate is and what the journey will look like. One of the good things about growing up is realizing that no matter how much planning you put into your life, what is supposed to happen is going to happen.

I do believe we have an element of control over the situations we find ourselves in, but how we get there has less to do with us as individuals and more to do with what the universe sees fit.

If someone were to ask me at twenty-three years old back in 2004 where I saw myself in five years, I would have said married to Marcus, living in a house in downtown Richmond where the houses have character and each one looks completely different from the one next to it. I also saw us with at least one kid by then, just happy and enjoying our family. In one short year, my goals, hopes, and dreams all changed—or became realized, depending on how you see life. I still wanted all of those things in five years, but I wanted them in a different way. I wanted them in addition to the happiness I had in my relationship with James, my career, and my friendships. I didn't want it because it would make my relationship better. My checklist changed for what I needed in a lifelong partner and I set out to find it—even if it was going to take longer than five years. In that moment, I felt I had found it with James.

How was Ayesha's timeline shaping up? She had gone from her job in Dallas—the city where her family lived, her friends were, and where it felt like home—to a new city and lifestyle. A few months ago, if you would have asked her where she saw herself in five years, she would have said, "Settled down with someone in Dallas." Whether for love or to make her parents happy, it did not matter. Now Ayesha was in love with a man who was from New York, who made life worth living, and was not Muslim. Time would only tell what would happen with these relationships. But in the meantime, we had other things to worry about. Like how we were going to afford living in New York for as much as it had to offer and still afford to eat!

Chapter 3

The Part-Time

New York, for those of you who have never lived there, is a very expensive city to live in. There are people who pay well over two thousand a month for a room, just to say they live in the city.

It's crazy! It is almost to the point where if you are not a rich banker with a big company or from a rich family where Daddy (or Mommy) is just handing down the money to their kids, there is no way you can enjoy all of the highlights of living in New York. With me paying eight hundred a month for a studio in Brooklyn and Ayesha paying anywhere from a thousand to twelve hundred a month for subleases around the city, and as two young girls only two years into our careers the only way we were going to be able to have any extra money was to get part-time jobs. I was sitting at my desk one day and my phone lit up. It was Ayesha.

"What are you doing?" she asked.

"Nothing" I answered. "You know, working...looking on Craigslist for a part-time job for us."

"Well, I think you can stop looking," she replied. "I have found one for us. We have an interview tonight. Well, I have an interview tonight. I called the number on the ad and left a message and he called me right back and said he is holding interviews tonight at six-thirty," she explained.

"Wait a second," I said, "do we even know what we will be doing?"

"He said it is a sales slash customer service position and we will learn more when we get there for the interview," Ayesha said. Apparently, that was enough information for me.

"Okay. So should I call him or just show up with you?" I asked.

"You should probably call him and let him know that you heard about the position and that you will come up there tonight," she advised.

I was all set to do that, but my day got really busy. For some reason when you want to accomplish something that has nothing to do with work, the workday seems to know and wants to dump a ton of things on you. Hours passed and suddenly it was six p.m.

Ayesha was freaking out because she thought we were going to be late and I was going through World War III and could not leave my desk. I had three big money schedules to get back to a few media buyers by their deadline of close of business that day and was almost done with the last one. So I told her, "Just go and I will meet you there."

"Did you call him and let him know you were coming?" she asked worriedly.

"No, I had no time to do that. I am just going to show up and see what happens—it will be fun!" I teased.

Forty-five minutes later I was running down Fulton Street looking for the building Ayesha texted me while I was on the train. I found it and discovered there were twenty floors and I had no clue what floor the interview was on. I looked at the directory for a clue and found a law office that sounded like they would be holding interviews. Don't ask me what the logic was behind this decision. I went to the office and found someone to ask.

"Hi. Is this where the interviews for the customer service position are?" I asked.

She was looking at me like I peed on myself.

"Did you guys post a listing on Craigslist for a part-time position?" I asked again in case I was not clear the first time. Still no response.

"Okay—thanks," I said as I went to the lobby to call Ayesha. She picked up but said nothing.

"Hello?" I said. She hung up on me. Okay. Knowing my best friend, the silence followed by the hang up meant she was about to text me the floor she was on but she couldn't talk just then. And boom—there was the text: 20th floor, suite 225. I walked into a small area with three or four different rooms. It looked like the air was going to be bad and they needed to open a window before I even walked into the space. I saw a small group of people huddled in a corner so I headed that way. Ayesha was sitting all the way in the back of the group—no doubt the first to arrive. I pulled up a chair and sat on the outside of the group. A man of average height was in front. He was wearing jeans that were tight around the stomach and a polo shirt with a popped collar. His name was John and he had this presence that made it hard to tell if he was gay or not. He talked very well and seemed happy to be in that tight, musty room. He was giving a description of the job as I got settled.

"The name of our organization is the Committee for a Unified Independent Party. What we do is help raise awareness of the candidates who are running as Independents, where they stand on issues, and what Independent voters can do to help. Our other job is to contact voters who are registered as Independents in New York as well as other states to make them aware that this organization exists and ask for their financial support to help us keep going," he explained.

As he continued, I gave Ayesha a look of bewilderment.

She had managed to find us a part-time job that paid ten dollars an hour plus commission that didn't sound half bad. She gave me a look that said, "I know!"

John continued with his agenda, "So if there are no more questions, I want to give all of you the script that we use on the cold call to inform Independent voters of who we are. We will take turns reading the portion that I give you to read, but with a twist. I want you to read the script as if you are the character I am going to assign you," he explained with a smile on his face.

What the fuck? He started the farthest from me with this older woman who had already annoyed everyone in the room during John's opening speech by asking way too many crazy questions for a situation like this. Her character was a professor at an Ivy League school. She read it as if someone really stuck a stick up her butt and twisted it. I think John was looking for a reason not to hire her. Then it was the next guy's turn. He looked about our age, twenty-fiveish, young, and looking for more money. He opened his mouth and it was a wreck. "Hello, isth John th-there?" he started. "Th-this isth Jamesth withs CUIP, a Committee for a Uni-unified Independent Par-party."

Why, why, why? Why would you come to an interview for sales and customer service where they warned us that we would be on the phones all night talking to people when you have a lisp that bad?

Now it was Ayesha's turn. She had to read it like she was an angry person. It made me laugh out loud when she put on the dramatic Ayesha. Soon it was my turn. I had to read it as if I were Oprah. Ayesha and I were in our own world with laughter.

If they did not pick up in the beginning that we knew each other, by that point, I think they all realized. So I cleared my throat and gathered up my best authoritative, excited, deep, emotional voice and channeled Oprah. She would have been very proud.

After the readings, John said he would be calling everyone very soon to let them know if they got the job. Ayesha and I decided to go to a nearby brewery that had great raspberry beer and awesome sliders. As we sat there and reminisced about all the crazy people we had just met, my cell phone rang. It was a number I did not recognize.

"Hello?" I answered.

"Can I speak with Farissa?" the voice on the other end asked.

"This is she," I responded in my serious voice that I could depend on not to sound beer-buzzed.

"Hi Farissa. This is John from CUIP. We want to offer you a position with us," he announced.

"Wow! That was fast. Great. I will take it," I said just as fast.

"Can you start tomorrow?" he asked me.

"Sure. What time do you need me in?" I asked, surprised this was all happening so fast.

"If you can make it in by six p.m., that would be great! Is Ayesha with you?" he asked, almost already knowing the answer to the question.

"Yeah she is right here, hold on," I answered as I handed her the phone, whispering that it was John.

John proceeded to tell Ayesha everything he just told me—and just like that we had part-time jobs.

The next night we were at the part-time office ready to work.

We met the group of people we would be working with, mostly older women who had been doing this for a long time as volunteers. We got our scripts and the binder full of sheets with names, phone numbers, and addresses. There were about twenty-five names per sheet and about twenty-five sheets in the book. We had to make as many phone calls as we could from six-thirty until nine. We had to keep track of how many people we called, how many people we actually got on the phone, how many people we got to give the entire pitch to, and how many people we got to either pledge they would send in money or actually give us money right there on the phone. As we went to start our first shift, John had some last words of advice for us.

"After many years of doing this, we found that the ratios normally work like this: you have to make an average of one hundred sixty phone calls each night to reach thirty people on the phone to be able to ask ten of them for a donation, for at least three of them to say yes," he explained. "If you have any questions while you are on the phones, just wave me down," he finished.

"We are going to kick ass!" I said to Ayesha. For some reason I was always the cheerleader in the relationship. After a couple of months had passed, we had both gotten a couple of donations on credit cards, pledges, and checks in the mail from donors. We were doing okay, but approaching the point of shoot-yourself-in-the-head boredom with the whole thing: the room, the people, the script, all of it.

"If I have to speak to one more idiot who hangs up on me, I am walking out," Ayesha said one night.

"I know," I replied, "this is the worst job ever. Half of these people don't even know what party they are registered under. And who in their right mind would give a stranger their credit card number over the phone?" I scolded.

"Do you want to quit?" Ayesha asked.

"We can't, we're poor, remember?" I said.

"Oh yeah. I hate everyone!" she said.

It was one of those Saturday mornings where James and I had had way too much to drink the night before. The room was spinning when I woke up and my mouth felt like I had been chewing on cotton balls all night—and to make matters worse, I had to be at my part-time job by nine a.m. and it was already eight-thirty. I took a five-minute shower, pulled back my hair, put on some lip gloss—because no matter how late you are, there should always be time for lip gloss—and ran to the train. By the time I got to the city I was already ten minutes late, so I decided to run into Starbucks for a cup of coffee. I got in the line and I was standing behind an equally hungover Ayesha.

"We are so late," I said.

"I know. And I don't even care," was Ayesha's response.

We had stopped caring about arriving on time a long time ago, due to the thirty-minute warm-up they did before we got on the phones. We figured as long as we didn't miss any phone time, we were good. We headed up in the elevator telling each other about our nights with our boyfriends and what led to us feeling so hungover.

"I was so drunk last night, I don't even remember if we had IC," I randomly explained to Ayesha. IC was our homemade abbreviation for intercourse.

"That is funny," she said. "Don't you think you would feel something this morning?" she asked.

As we pondered that and walked through the door leading to the worst Saturday morning ever, all I could think was that there better be no drama that morning. I was hungover, tired, and about to start my period. That was the last place I wanted to be just then. I just wanted to be left alone to enjoy my coffee.

As we walked in, it was clear we had not been missed. All of the women over fifty that we worked with were very chipper for nine a.m.

and were talking about haircuts, ugly sweaters, and what was for lunch—just weird. We sat down at our posts and waited for instructions to start. Just as John told everyone it was time to get on the phones, one of the volunteers walked in the door. She looked like she had been crying for hours. Immediately everyone was looking at her wondering what was wrong, and I knew Ayesha and I were thinking the same thing. Why would you still come into this job if something was THAT wrong with you?

She found a seat and one of the women went over to her to see what was wrong. Before she leaned in to ask the crying lady what was wrong, she made sure to look at Ayesha and I with a motion that meant 'keep dialing.' So Ayesha and I pretended to dial numbers so we could listen to what was going on. This is a technique we learned to perfect one night when we were having so much fun talking to each other, the people who actually answered their phones were getting on our nerves interrupting our conversation. So we decided to dial all the digits of the number except the last one so it looked like we had dialed a whole phone number and we were waiting for someone to pick up. When the busy signal got too loud in our ears, we would hang up and fake-dial again.

"Is everything okay?" The woman asked the girl who was crying. "If you need someone to talk to, we are here for you. What is it?" she pressed.

"Oh, I'm a mess. Do you have any tissue?" she asked.

She took a tissue from her friend and blew her nose like we were all family.

"I just got some bad news last night. The doctor called and said that Misty died," she explained.

"Oh, honey, I am so sorry. You must be a mess. If you want to go home for the day we will understand," our team leader offered.

"No, it feels better to get out of the house. When I am there, all I can think about is the fact that Misty is not there," she said.

"Come here," our leader commanded.

She embraced her with love so strong that I think I even felt a little bit of a burn in my right eye. Our red-headed team leader, who had been comforting the woman who obviously just had a death in the family, came back to the table, very happy to see that Ayesha and I were still dialing through the drama.

"Is she okay?" Ayesha asked, putting us into full investigation mode. "Was it a death in the family?"

"Yeah, her cat died yesterday," she explained.

What? All of this drama so early on a Saturday morning like her mother passed away because her cat died? And I am allowed to be annoyed by this because I have a cat that I love and would be sad if he died, but not to the point where I would need moral support to make it through my shift at my part-time job.

As Ayesha and I were communicating this to each other with our eyes, our nonverbal conversation was interrupted by an outburst of tears. One of the woman's friends had heard the news and came out of her office to comfort her friend. As she approached her, the woman who had just lost her cat threw up her arms to expose two underarms full of hair and sweat rings. I was so done with these people.

Chapter 4

"I Hate Everyone."
"They're Stupid." "You're Dumb."

There comes a time at every job where you get into a routine. What time you go outside for your cigarettes, what time you get lunch, who you eat your lunch with, and the people you go for drinks with. Ayesha and I had been working at Interep for about eight months and we were cranking. We had our account lists, we were making our goals, our bosses loved us; we were just not making any money because we were still in our first year. At least once a week we would sit down and strategize on how we were going to get the raise we wanted for that next year. We were set! We were the "twins" at work not to be messed with. Then we got the news that someone who had been working out in the Los Angeles office was moving back to New York.

Enter Stephanie.

Stephanie was from Pittsburgh, but you would never guess it. She had the whole "valley girl from California" thing down. She was not a blonde—hated blondes, in fact—but had "blonde moments." She had been working for Interep for six or seven years when we met her. She started in the New York office and then after a year or so of that was transferred to the Philadelphia office, and then after a couple of years there she was transferred to the Los Angeles office. During her time in outside offices, she worked for the new business development team in the company, targeting different agencies that did not have a business relationship with us and persuading them to use us when buying radio. Well, the network department, the department Ayesha worked in, was growing and they needed some more people to cover the workload, so Stephanie was called in and she jumped at the opportunity to move back to the best city on earth.

Things started off okay. We really didn't know her that well, so conversations were limited to "hi" and "bye" and work-related things. We would stop talking if she walked into the room if we were talking about something personal—because it was personal. But then we started to notice something.

Stephanie would come into Ayesha's office when she saw both of us in there just to stand and talk.

"Oh sorry, did I interrupt?" asked Stephanie.

"It's okay. We were just talking. What did you need?" Ayesha would ask in her matter of fact way.

"Oh well, if you guys want me to come back when you are done—I can," Stephanie would answer, testing the waters.

Ayesha and I would give each other the look that said, "What is wrong with this girl?" That was my cue to go back to my office.

That was the first glimpse we had into Stephanie's personality.

Over the next few weeks it became evident that Stephanie liked us and wanted to be a part of the fun that was obvious Ayesha and I were having every time we spoke to each other. I told Ayesha it was not nice to be mean on purpose so we needed to include her on a more personal level.

Right around the time this decision was made, Stephanie decided to have her first panic attack since being back in New York. Work was getting very busy and deadlines were coming up and we all were busy. Ayesha and I are very laid back people. We do what needs to be done, when it needs to be done, and keep it calm while doing it. So our reaction to a panic attack was probably less than desired.

Sometime later, we were all in Ayesha's office just talking as we often did. Ayesha is not an only child, but she can have "only child tendencies" at times. Her true friends understand this and it is one of the things we add to the list of things we love about her because it can be very humorous. Others, well Stephanie, took her literally quite a lot.

"So what do we want to get for lunch?" Ayesha asked me one day in the office.

"I don't know," I said. "What about Wendy's? I could go for a single with cheese!"

"That does sound good. I could get the chicken sandwich that I love," said Ayesha.

"Good, so let's go," we agreed.

Then in walked Stephanie. "Where are you guys going for lunch today? I'll come with..." she tested again.

I always let Ayesha answer questions that we both knew the answer to. I also always wanted her to tell stories to a group of people if they were interested in something that had just happened to us. I always felt like, "if you wanted to know, you should have been there."

"We're going to Wendy's—let's go," is all Ayesha said.

"I don't want Wendy's," Stephanie said. "What else can we get?" she asked.

"I hate you!" Ayesha said in the way she always did. "Now we have to pick a place all over again," she jokingly complained.

That was the second thing!

Stephanie had a habit of coming in late. Sometimes it would be later than others, but she was always late. We all had to get to work by eight-thirty a.m. Ayesha would get there at seven-thirty because she is a morning person and just crazy. I would get there around eight-forty every morning—unless there was a meeting. Sometimes we would look up at about nine-thirty and realize that we had not seen Stephanie all morning. Every time this happened, Stephanie would come steamrolling in and her first stop would be Ayesha's office to tell her the story of what made her late that morning. Every morning it was something different. One day it would be the bus's fault. It was not running on time. Other times it would be the train's fault. They were delayed that morning. One morning it was the rain. It was raining so hard that she was late.

One particular morning Ayesha had had enough. She hated that Stephanie felt she needed to explain to her why she was late every morning. She was not her boss, she did not sign her paychecks, Stephanie made way more money than we both did. Ayesha wanted to say, "If you want to be late, be late—just stop lying to me like I'm stupid!" But she actually said out loud, "Why do you do this every morning?"

"What?" Stephanie asked, confused.

"Come running in here as soon as you get to work to tell me a long story instead of going to your office, starting up your computer, and working?" Ayesha scolded.

"Well if you don't like me coming into your office, I will stop. You didn't have to catch an attitude, you could have just told me," Stephanie said, shaking.

"It's not about coming into my office," explained Ayesha, "it's about the long song and dance that comes with it every morning. I have stuff to do!"

That was the third thing!

At this point, Stephanie's feelings were hurt, so in true social weirdness form, she called a meeting. We all had to sit down together behind closed doors so she could tell us how she was feeling. She basically told us that she felt like we were trying to exclude her from things we were doing and that we could be harsh at times when we spoke to her (or maybe that was just me) and that we should include her in things that we do or just let her know if we don't want to be her friend. Ayesha allowed me to take the lead on that one because it was new information that needed to be shared on our behalf. Ayesha was good at communicating the things we had already talked about. We were comfortable with our roles.

"Stephanie, I just want to let you know that if we have hurt your feelings, we did not mean to. Ayesha and I have been friends for a year and we have inside jokes, we have stories, and we do things outside of work. None of these things are done to make you feel bad—it is not about you." Maybe that was that "harsh" thing she was talking about. But it was the truth. Ayesha decided to assist.

"What I think Farissa is trying to say," Ayesha said, "is that we are sorry if we hurt your feelings. We did not mean to. But you don't have to over-analyze every situation. We are just having a good time. Just relax—and try not to take everything so personally," she pleaded.

The conversation went on for the next half hour or so. By the end of it we were all okay. We were friends. It led to many more times we were annoyed and pissed off at Stephanie, but it also led to many times when we weren't. At that moment, Stephanie became someone we really cared about.

As different as all women are, we all pretty much have the same way of communicating. We like to get it out in the open and share our feelings so that we are all on the same page. Men, on the other hand—how do they say—are from Mars!

James and I were a year and a couple months into our relationship. It was September of 2006. It was still nice and hot on the East Coast and New York felt great. He had been working really hard for the past couple of months, coming home at one or two in the morning from work and getting up at seven and doing it all over again—including some weekends! It was looking like he would have a free weekend coming up soon and he wanted to do something fun. We had wanted to make it to the beach. Summer was almost over and I had not once put on a bathing suit.

"Let's rent a car," James said one night as we lay naked in bed on top of the covers. It was so hot in his little apartment all we could do was lay still in front of the window, not move, and hope for a breeze.

"We could get the car for the weekend and just drive somewhere before the summer is over," he said in a day-dreamy tone. I loved the idea!

"Where would we go?" I asked.

"Anywhere you want to go—let's just get out of the city. What about D.C.?" he asked with a smirk.

"That would be nice," I said smiling, "but what if we keep going and go to Virginia Beach? We have not been to the beach all summer. We could stop in Richmond and I could introduce you to people, show you where I went to high school, and we could spend some time on the beach. It would be so much fun. A road trip!" I said.

"Yeah, that would be fun," he said. "I'll rent the car and we'll leave Friday," he said decidedly.

Looking back now, I laugh because I acted like such a girl. But sometimes we can't help it—especially when we REALLY like a guy. The whole week at work I was telling people that that weekend James and I would be driving down to Virginia Beach and stopping in Richmond and he would meet my parents. I was on cloud nine that whole week.

Friday finally came and I had a rough day at work. I was supposed to get out early. James had taken the day off and I kept getting busier and busier all day, so we didn't wind up hitting the road until much later than we'd planned. Earlier in the week we had expanded the trip to three stops. The plan was: Friday drive to D.C. and stop to visit James's sister who had just moved there.

Then we would wake up in the morning and head to Richmond on Saturday. We would spend the day in Richmond and drive to the beach at night so we could spend the whole of Sunday at the beach and then drive all the way back to New York on Sunday night. At least it sounded like a good idea when we came up with it.

"We are probably not going to make it to D.C. until ten or eleven tonight," James stated once we finally got on the road. "I don't just want to get there, go to sleep, and then leave. I haven't seen my sister in a year." James was concerned about the planning of our trip. All I heard was "You will not be able to introduce me to your parents."

"What about this?" I suggested. "We can hang out in D.C. tomorrow and head to Richmond in the evening. I really want you to get a chance to meet my parents." As soon as I said it, it was like all the sound in the world disappeared. The silence in the car lasted so long that I wanted to disappear into thin air.

He finally found something to say.

"I thought you said you wanted to show me around Richmond—where you went to high school; maybe go out for a drink with some of your friends," he said with the least amount of feeling I had ever felt from James.

"And introduce you to my parents!" I interjected. I had never really said that exact phrase, but he was supposed to know that taking him to Richmond where both of my parents resided, and where my brother and sister lived, would mean meeting my family, too.

"Why would I drive all the way to Richmond, give you a tour of the city, and not at least stop into my parent's house? Does that even sound normal to you? What did you think was going to happen—I would leave you at the hotel and go say 'hi' to my parents and tell them you decided to stay at the hotel because you are not ready to meet them? That makes me look like a dumbass!" I said, meaning every word.

We didn't speak for the next thirty minutes. All I could do was look out the window and cry. And then came the question of all questions. He asked, "What's wrong?"

What's wrong? What's wrong? Then I gave him his answer.

"What's wrong? My boyfriend just told me he doesn't want to meet my parents and we are on our way to where my parents live. I have told my mom I am coming to see her this weekend and I am bringing my boyfriend. I told all of my friends at work that my boyfriend and I are going to Richmond this weekend and he is going to meet my family. Now, when I get to work on Monday, everyone is going to want to know how it was and I have no idea what I am going to tell them. THAT is what's wrong!" I shrieked through my sobbing.

"Don't worry about it though," I interjected before he could say anything. "If you don't want to meet my parents, you don't have to meet them. I truly do not want you doing something you do not want to do. We don't even have to go to Richmond—we can just stay with YOUR sister all weekend in D.C. and do stuff with her and her husband!" I said, finally stopping for air.

I was so hurt! There were few things that have happened to me that have made me feel like that. We again had a long silent pause that felt nothing like the first time. He finally had something to say.

"You keep saying that I don't want to meet your family. It is not that. I just want to meet them when I am ready. Just because I am not ready to meet them doesn't mean I love you any less. I love you! I just want it to be the right time. Can you understand that?" he asked me.

"I can understand that," I said. "But can you understand that I don't think that if you meet my parents it means you are asking my dad for my hand in marriage. You are making a much bigger deal about this than it needs to be. You should have just said 'no' to Virginia Beach and Richmond," I said more calmly this time.

"You are right. I should have said not this time, maybe another time. But you are wrong about one thing—if it wasn't such a big deal, you wouldn't be so hurt and upset right now!" he said.

I had to admit to myself that he had a point, but I was not ready to let him know that. "You wanna stop at this Waffle House?" he asked.

"Sure," was all I said.

Chapter 5

Random

If you look up the definition of friend in the dictionary, it will read: "A person you know well and regard with affection and trust." That could not be any truer for how Ayesha and I felt about each other. We spoke ten times a day at this stage in our life. We could not start our workday without a quick synopsis of the previous night. It was fun! It was nonstop fun. Everywhere we went and everything we did, we came back with a story. It was almost too good to be true that both of us decided to move for work and love, and had found a best friend in each other. It was like being in seventh grade with a BFF all over again, and boy did we live it up!

It was one of those days where you feel like you are sinning if you are inside. The sun was shining, the temperature was set on perfect, and all we wanted to do was go somewhere. So lunchtime finally came and we decided we were going to go shopping. We took the shuttle across town to Times Square and walked toward Madison Square Garden. As a New Yorker, it always seems like a good idea to go for a walk—until you get there and remember that eight million other people had the same idea, plus three million of their closest friends who live out of town.

We were walking and I don't even think we knew what our specific destination was. All of a sudden, I heard someone yell out: "Free Maury Povich tickets. Get your free tickets to today's taping."

I looked at Ayesha and she looked like she did not hear the girl. So I grabbed her. "Did you hear that? Free Maury tickets. Let's go!"

We started our sideways dart toward the other end of the street—an action that Ayesha would later describe as me pushing her into the Maury studios.

"Do you guys have any tickets left?" I asked the lady at the door.

"We sure do. But they are for the taping that starts in ten minutes," she answered.

Ayesha and I looked at each other still thinking that it was a good idea. It was 12:50 in the afternoon. Depending on how long the taping was, we could stay and not be missed at work—it was a slow day anyway.

"How long is the show?" I asked.

"Well, you would have to be in your seat until two p.m. and we can't let anyone out until we are done," she answered.

"Okay, give us a second," I said.

I was all about it. I had just gotten the new Blackberry! If I got an e-mail, I would be able to reply to whoever needed me and they wouldn't even know I wasn't at my desk. Ayesha, on the other hand, was not as lucky.

"I don't have a Blackberry. If Bruce e-mails me, I won't know until we get back—and what if it's important?" she contemplated.

"You are right," I reinforced. "I guess we should do the right thing—until next time." And we walked on looking for the next crazy opportunity. A month later, an article about Maury cheating on his wife with a stripper "mysteriously" appeared on my desk. I had forgotten all about that day, but Ayesha knew I would get it right away.

As busy as we were at work sometimes, there were other times where there was nothing to do there. So to keep from falling into comatose, we would look for fun, cheap, things to do in the city on different websites. One of our favorite websites was Craigslist. It was just starting to explode and people were posting things left and right on the site. Odd jobs they needed filled, items for sale, events happening, anything that you could think of was on there. We would spend hours a day on that thing just looking at how crazy people were. Ayesha would send me a link to something she would find that was sick, funny, or just plain wrong.

The Craigslist obsession really started when we were looking for a part-time job, then once we found that, we started looking for free stuff and events. Of course, Ayesha would have to come across the weirdest guy in New York offering something for free.

"Here, open up this link and tell me if you think this is weird," was the instant message that popped up on my screen from Ayesha. I opened the link, which read: Unlimited Free Pedicures for a Woman. The ad went on to read: "I love feet! It is that simple. If you let me take you to a spa and watch the women give you a pedicure and when she is done let me rub your feet, I will pay for your pedicure—as many times as you want." I just sat there with my mouth open for a minute astonished that this guy was walking the streets of New York and that Ayesha needed my opinion on whether or not this was weird. I picked up the phone and dialed her extension.

"Yeah?" she said.

"You want to know if this is weird? Hello! A stranger wants to take you to get a pedicure and then wants to watch and touch your feet afterwards? Um, yes, very weird," I said still not sure why I even had to answer, but amused nonetheless.

"But we will be in a public place. It's not like he wants to give me the pedicure," she tried to justify.

"Yeah, but when you are done and want to walk by yourself to the train, who is to say he is not going to follow you? And what would Steve say if he knew what you did?" I asked, trying to infuse some common sense into this conversation.

"You are right, you are right! I hate you!" she said.

"Yes I know—you hate me because I am right. Glad I could talk you off the ledge!"

Ever since J.Lo told us how she used to get back and forth from the Bronx to the city, I have been a fan. She is by no means the best singer in the world. No one would call her the best actress either, but she has an awesome business sense, is gorgeous, has great fashion sense, can dance her ass off, and she is from the Bronx—need I say more? I have to watch or listen to anything that has anything to do with J.Lo. Ayesha used to make fun of me for this but I really didn't care. All these years later, look whose career has stood the test of time! Anyway…

It was July 24th, 2006, J.Lo's birthday, and in an effort to have a great happy hour, we decided to dedicate it to Jennifer Lopez. I had a J.Lo jean jacket that I got in college (that I JUST retired a couple years ago) that I was going to wear for the day.

Ayesha was going to play J.Lo hits all day on the computer and we would go out and drink to celebrate, secretly hoping that we would run into her somewhere that night. It's New York, right? You never know.

So the day progressed. We did our work and everything was as normal as it could be. I had recently signed up for this invitation company where you fill out a form of things that interest you, tell them what city you live in, and they send you invitations to events that fit your taste and budget. So, of course, today of all days, J.Lo's birthday, I would have to get my first invitation to an event—and a free one at that. It was a sales event with unknown—I mean up and coming—designers from New York. The designers would be there with their line. There would be free cocktails and snacks, and there were going to be live models walking around with the designers' pieces on.

Ayesha and I were in a place where we never turned down free cocktails. That would be crazy! There was no reason why we couldn't celebrate J.Lo's birthday looking at new clothing lines and drinking free drinks. I also knew that Ayesha was only doing the J.Lo happy hour for me, so we went to the fashion show. It was great having so many options to have a good time.

By the end of the fashion show, we had seen a new line of formal dresses, a new line of Indian-designed handbags, tasted catfish and sweet potatoes from a cool new soul food restaurant downtown, and got asked by one of the designers –who happened to be my favorite—to model in one of his shows.

We never did, but that's not the point.

It was one of those days at work. It was gloomy outside and even grayer in the office. It was a slow day and five-thirty p.m. could not come fast enough. Ayesha and I were on a mission to find something to do that night, so we would have something to look forward to. We focused our attention on, you guessed it, Craigslist. One thing that we always kept in mind was that not everyone on this website was telling the truth about what they were selling or what they were willing to trade. You couldn't always trust the pictures either because people would take pictures from another website and post it like it was the picture of the product they were selling. It only took an hour or so before I came across the ad.

"Huge Celebrity Bash Tonight at Hip Downtown Bar." It promised people like Paris Hilton and many more celebrities. It was the week before the Video Music Awards and they were being held in New York that year. So there were a lot of famous people in the city at that time. The ad promised that all we had to do to gain access to these two tickets to the event was show up at the door and say that we were on the author of the ad's guest list. She had one spot left and it was first come first serve. I sent the link directly to Ayesha.

"This would have been so much fun to do, but she only has one spot left," I told Ayesha once she called me.

"We can still go! She is not collecting names. She is just telling people to call her and then the spot is taken. If we call her and take the last spot and show up early, we will beat the other people she promised the spot to. It's perfect!" Ayesha explained to me. The funny thing is she had me thinking this was a good idea. We thought about it some more and convinced ourselves it would work.

"But what would we wear? If we go to a thing like this and actually get in, we might rub elbows with really important people, so we have to look sharp," I explained as we thought it over some more.

"I know. I have a dress that I have been dying to wear and this would be the perfect place to wear it," Ayesha replied enthusiastically.

"Look outside. It looks like it is going to pour down any second. What if it rains?" I asked.

"Then we won't go—but only if it rains," was the deal she put on the table.

"What if we get all dressed up and get to the party and the spots on her guest list are full? We would have done all this for nothing." I was sure this question would make her see this plan was flawed. I wasn't as in love with this plan as Ayesha was.

There were too many question marks for me.

"That is why we are showing up early so we can beat the other people who know about the spots on this girl's list," was her answer, but it still did nothing for my mood.

"Well, how are we going to get there early when I have to go all the way to Brooklyn, shower, change, and meet you at your house? By then it would already be eight or eight-thirty," I said, almost sure I was close to getting her on my side, which is crazy since I was the one who sent her the link. But Ayesha's determination was not going anywhere. I think it was the chance that she could catch a glimpse of Jessica Simpson that kept her so determined. Seriously! She was a huge fan. If you know anything about Jessica Simpson and the early 2000s, it was the height of her marriage to Nick and their reality show years.

"If it is raining when we leave work, we will not go!" she said decidedly and that ended the conversation.

At five p.m., the sky opened up and it poured all night long!

By now we were well into 2006 and Ayesha and I had become inseparable. We were in constant communication throughout the day, we were able to finish each other's sentences, and we could communicate a complete thought to each other from across the room without saying a word. On Friday afternoons, when it was time to go home, if we did not speak to each other the entire weekend no one was upset. We just had this unspoken rule; weekends were for the boyfriends.

We had so much fun during the week with work, the part-time, happy hours, fashion shows, sample sales, work events, and whatever, that by the time Friday night rolled around, it was time to spend some quality time with our boyfriends and we were perfectly fine with that. That is why we should have known that joining this book club was going to be a mistake. The first sign: they wanted to have their meetings on Sunday afternoons at two.

We thought it would be fun to meet other girls. They were all in our industry. Some of them were buyers at agencies in the city and either bought print, radio, or television advertising for the clients their agency had. One of the girls was a buyer for Lacoste. Her entire closet was one name brand—it was actually a little scary. Ayesha had met one of the girls through work. She was one of the buyers that Ayesha had worked with recently.

The first book was by Jill A. Davis. We had a week to read it because Ayesha told me a week before the meeting that we were part of this new club. I had no problem reading the book in a week. It was a great book. It was about a woman who had issues with herself and falling in love. She had a hard time allowing herself to just be in the moment and learning how to grow and love herself before anyone else could love her. It focussed on the women that were her friends and the weekly poker game they had at her house. It showed how much each one of their lives changed throughout the story and how much both the women and the readers learned about the women by the end of each poker game. I would still recommend it today.

So Ayesha and I got to the girl's apartment on the Upper East Side at two p.m. I was excited at the thought of having drinks in the middle of the afternoon and talking about this cute book I just read. We were one of the first waves of girls to show up since Ayesha always has to be on time. We got a tour of the apartment and a breeze-through of what everyone's name was.

The living room was small so we staked out seats right away. More people started to show up, the snacks came out, and we watched to see what everyone wanted to drink. One of the girls who actually lived in the apartment said, "I guess we should have gotten some wine for this. That would have been fun!"

Um, yes. I looked at Ayesha with disbelief. No wine? I had to take a shower, get dressed, and leave my boyfriend laying on the couch in his sexy boxer briefs with the windows open and the slight breeze of Brooklyn, and there is no wine!

"So…who was able to finish the book?" asked the leader of the pack. There were about ten girls sitting in her tight living room and five of them, including me, were able to say we finished the book. How come I was taking this book club more seriously than the people actually in the club? So we talked about the book for a while and made suggestions for what the next book should be and then magically the conversation turned, as it always does with women everywhere, to where we are all from, boys, sex, and tampons.

By the end of the afternoon, we had learned that all of those girls were from the Midwest and had been to school almost all in the same area, majored in the same thing, and moved to New York to make it big in advertising. None of them had ever been off the island of Manhattan during their time in New York.

One of the girls used to work for a free clinic back home and told us one too many stories about girls who came in with "boyfriend" stories. One of the other girls, who was twenty-seven, was a virgin and was terrified at the thought of having sex. The best part was that one of the other girls, who was twenty-eight, had never worn a tampon, had promised herself that she would never wear a tampon, and would rather wear two pads before she put a tampon in—and she was on a softball team. Needless to say, we never attended another book club meeting!

Chapter 6

Brooklyn

Earlier in the year, I had made one of my dreams come true: I moved into my own apartment—the first apartment that was mine and all mine! No one else's name was on the lease.

The only person who would see if it was dirty was me. I could walk around in my worst outfit and not shower for a day. I could eat cereal for dinner every night. And the scariest thing of all—the bills were all mine, too.

It happened right around the time the Rapper class was ending. I knew for sure that I was going to be able to stay in New York. I couldn't wait to start looking for my place. I had already done some research about neighborhoods that I could afford, and there weren't too many. The main things that I wanted to keep in mind were: proximity to work, trains, and James. Adding up all of these elements put me right in Brooklyn. The Bronx was affordable on my budget and it was where I grew up, but the commute to work and anywhere else in the city was going to take forever. I couldn't afford anything in the city unless it was in an area that would make my skin crawl. So I narrowed it down. I knew from working out a budget that I had anywhere from seven hundred to eight hundred and fifty a month to spend on rent. Depending on where you live, that might sound like a lot of money, but in New York, that was (and still is) chump change. What my eight hundred a month got me in 2006 was a nice size studio apartment in Crown Heights, Brooklyn. I had a nice size entryway with ugly tile flooring, an eat-in kitchen with the same ugly floor, an oven that didn't work for the entire time I lived there, a bathroom with everything I needed including an area for Buddy Snuggles's litter box. Then there was the "living area." It was enough for me to fit my queen size bed that I had received from my parents as my college graduation gift, two end tables with lamps that I had stolen from my dad months ago, a tall dresser that was part of that original bedroom set from my parents, a floor lamp, a love seat I got from The Dump, a coffee table, and a nineteen-inch television on an entertainment stand in the corner. It was my favorite area of the apartment.

During the day, the sun would pour into the living area and hit the white cement walls and make it the brightest space. There was so much more that I wanted, but there was so much that I had to be grateful for! This was the reason why I had to leave Richmond—leave Marcus. I had to be able to look back on life and say I was able to make it on my own, in my own apartment, with no help. I knew that if I became a wife and mother before I could say this was true about myself, I was not going to be happy. It was the noisiest place I have ever lived, and I secretly wished that I lived with James in Brooklyn Heights in his brownstone apartment overlooking the Promenade—but I didn't. I lived in MY apartment—for a year, anyway!

I loved Brooklyn immediately. What was not to love?

Every neighborhood had something unique about it. Brooklyn Heights, where James lived, was at the tip of the borough. It is the side that is closest to Manhattan. Since he worked downtown, he was one stop away from work no matter what train he decided to take that morning. Brooklyn Heights is very historic. It has brownstones, which were once single-family homes that have been converted into apartment buildings with views of the Statue of Liberty and the Brooklyn Bridge. It has a cute bistro on almost every corner and you can walk and walk for hours before you realize you are tired.

Crown Heights, where my apartment was, is very different. The first thing to know is that Crown Heights was a very popular place for black people from the Caribbean to come live as they all migrated to the States. There were so many accents in my neighborhood, I sometimes felt like I was in another country. I could get jerk chicken at any hour of the night and go to the fish market or the meat market everyday to get fresh meat to make for dinner. There were no restaurants or cute bistros, but there was a park across the street from my building where I schooled James a couple of times on the handball court—with witnesses! There were laundry mats, liquor stores, and men on every corner creatively telling me how attractive they thought I was.

No matter where we were in Brooklyn, we had a great time. There was no reason to leave Brooklyn on the weekends. There was so much going on during the summer. There was a free concert series at the park in Fort Green and we got to see the Sugar Water Festival that summer. It was a concert featuring Queen Latifah, Erykah Badu, and Jill Scott. It was one of the best summers ever.

The other thing that Brooklyn had that we were hard-pressed to find in other places in New York were Black people—and I don't mean just any Black people—but all kinds of Black people. There were people who had just moved from the Islands the year before who were learning and adjusting to life in a different country. There were young people trying to make it in their careers, there were people who had money and lived in some of the biggest, nicest brownstones right next door to the white people, and much, much more. It just felt good to be able to go into a high-end restaurant and look around and have more than half of the tables look just like me. And then go to a poetry club later that night and listen to talented people read things from their heart and have it be about the same issue I faced last Friday at work. Or go to the bar on the corner to see the line waiting to get in full of good looking brothers in nice jeans, blazers, and chic city shoes—brothers!

And last but certainly not least, NO TOURISTS asking how to get somewhere! I could have lived in Brooklyn forever.

Chapter 7

How Can We Make More Money? "I'm Poor."

That whole first year was a hustle for Ayesha and me. We were living and working in the big city, eating out as much as we could, drinking as much as we could, and shopping as much as we could. We were spending the little bit of money that we made faster than we could make it. But we were having fun! There was not a week that went by that we didn't discuss our strategy for making more money next year, when we were going to talk to our bosses, how much money we were going to ask for, and what was the least amount of money we would settle for. All these things needed to be worked out before we set up any meetings.

One day we decided to break out the calculator and put a dollar amount to what we thought we should be making next year. This was really Ayesha's area of expertise. She was good with numbers and percentages and figuring out if we made a certain amount of money, which tax bracket that would put us in and how much our take-home would be. I just took her word for it and went with it.

"Okay," she said at one of our money meetings, "we currently both make $35,000 a year and our checks every two weeks are $993. Before taxes and health insurance, our checks should be somewhere around— hold on—$1,458. So that is sixty-eight percent. So let's say we tell them we want to make $50,000 next year. That means that our checks every two weeks before taxes and health insurance would be somewhere around $2,083. But that sixty-eight percent that we have to accommodate for now would probably go up with the raise because that might put us into a different tax bracket. So let's say we have to take out seventy-four percent. That would make our take-home checks about $1,540 every two weeks. That is a good number!" she finished as she took a breath. She was so on top of things.

"Yes, that is a good number," I said. "That's us bringing home about $500 more each check."

"That sounds right," she confirmed. "But what we should do is start off a little bit higher than $50,000 and ask for $55,000 or $60,000 because they will probably want to talk us down to $50,000 from that point. We just know that $50,000 is the least amount we will go for," she said.

I was empowered! It was just the conversation we needed to help us make it to the next payday. It worked every time.

In addition to our full-time jobs and our part-time jobs, we were still constantly on Craigslist trying to look for something to do or experience that would be the perfect surprise as soon as we saw it.

As these things go, one day I was on the website and I got inspired to write my own ad to see if I could get any clients of my own.

I was a pro at the website, so I knew all the proper steps to take to make this happen. The first step was to figure out what you were going to sell, offer, or make available to the public. What could I do that would not be scary and would make me money? It had to be something that I would be comfortable doing and that James wouldn't mind me doing once he found out about it. Nothing came to mind so I decided to contemplate the next important thing about a Craigslist ad—it had to be something that other people would be willing to spend money on. What do people spend money on that I could do for them or with them and get paid for it? And then it hit me: exercise!

I had wanted to start working out again. I just didn't have the money, time, or energy to get it done by myself. So if I felt that way, I'm sure there were other people who felt the same way. There were plenty of rich people who paid a lot of money to hire people to make them work out! That was it. I was going to put an ad on Craigslist to be a personal workout buddy. It was genius!

It only took a couple of minutes for me to get the ad up online. The best thing about this plan was that posting an ad on Craigslist was free, so I would hopefully make money and not even have to spend any money to do so. The ad was simple and true to Craigslist form and format: ARE YOU LOOKING TO BE IN THE BEST SHAPE OF YOUR LIFE? I WILL HELP YOU GET THERE!

I just knew that this was going to be the way I would make extra dough and make the stress of never having enough money go away. Now that the ad was up and running, I decided to let Ayesha in on the idea.

"Guess what?" I messaged her once it was posted.

"What?" Ayesha replied, with some hesitation.

"I put an ad on Craigslist," I said.

"Ha ha ha. For what?" she asked.

"To be an Exercise Buddy." Just typing it made me laugh so hard.

"Are you crazy? What is an Exercise Buddy?" she asked me with zero judgment.

"Here, I will send you the link." I brought up my ad as if I were a customer and copied and pasted it into Ayesha's IM screen. She read it.

"It actually sounds really good," she said.

That is why we are friends. She was proud of my Craigslist ad to be an Exercise Buddy for a negotiated fee.

"Thanks. I made it sound like I was really professional. I should get at least one hit," I said with hope.

"Let me know, psycho," was her response.

When you post an ad on Craigslist, they inform you that the ad will remain online for seven days and then it will be removed. If you want it up for longer, you have to re-post. I decided that if no one responded in a week, it just was not meant to be. I had the link set up to my personal e-mail address so all interested parties would send e-mails to my Yahoo account and I could reply at my own free will. Each morning, as usual, I checked my Yahoo account in the hope of finding someone interested in this newfound service I discovered I could provide.

Day seven just happened to be a Monday and I just knew that over the weekend someone had replied and wanted to hire me. Monday morning—zero hits!

A couple weeks had gone by and my first failed business idea was a forgotten memory. We had other things to talk about. "How much would your boss have to promise to pay you before you sleep with him just one time?" Ayesha asked one day, just when I thought there was nothing else she could say that would shock me.

"Well, Ayesha, it really depends on who my boss is. My current boss's bill would be pretty high," I replied in ALL seriousness. The president of the rep firm that I worked for was a short, white, forty-something-year-old guy from Brooklyn. You never knew if he was happy or angry and he made it so that you really didn't care—you just wanted to get your job done.

"No, really! Would one-hundred thousand for an annual salary be enough for you to do it?" she asked.

Okay. I could tell she really wanted to have this conversation, so I indulged her. "Well, that is a really nice amount of money and I would do a lot of things to make that money, but after you slept with him, even just the one time, would he still be your boss? Because if I had to be reminded of the nasty thing I did to get the raise every morning when I walked into work, I would kill myself." That was my truth.

"Yep. Let's say you knew that you would have to still see him every-day after you did it, what would your number be?" she asked again.

"I would say I would need a raise to an annual salary of two-hundred and fifty-thousand and I would need to make sure you got the same amount. If one of us was going to do this, both of us should benefit. I would want you to be in the room as well so you would have to see it and have the same memory," I said.

"Ew, that would be nasty!" she said in a tone of shock.

"Oh, so pimping me off to my boss is not gross, but you being there while it happens is nasty. I thought we were friends," I replied, to her disgust.

We talked back and forth about it for a while, sometimes having to stop to swallow some throw up. Right when we decided we were done with the conversation and we had done all we could without making ourselves sick, Ayesha's boss walked by her office and we both laughed so hard we cried all the way to lunch!

"Why do I only have ten dollars to my name and we don't get paid for another two days?" I asked Ayesha one day.

I was really confused as to how this could happen. It was a "good" pay period, too. Meaning, it was the fifteenth of the month pay cycle, so the only bills I had paid with my previous check were my credit cards and ComEd. It was typically the end of the month that was the struggle. Almost my whole $993 check went toward paying my rent and then I lived on what was left. So I was super confused why cash seemed low.

"Well what did you buy this week?" Ayesha wanted to know.

"Nothing really," I said. "Just the normal stuff: food, alcohol, snacks. I must be leaving something out," I said as I tried to retrace my steps.

What I was forgetting was that James had been away on business for the past four days and I had been left to take care of myself for breakfast, lunch, and the meal that I didn't realize would put such a dent in my wallet: dinner.

I knew that James took really good care of me and when we went out to dinner or ordered takeout, he would take care of it most times. But was I so dependent on him that when he was out of town for a few days, I felt it in my pocketbook? Apparently so.

Here I was, wondering where all the money had gone. It was a sad realization. Of course this was something I had to discuss further with Ayesha.

"How should I feel about this? On one hand, I am happy that I have a man that has the ability to take care of me and, more importantly, actually does. He loves me and he knows where I am financially so he does not expect a lot of a monetary contribution from me. I try to do really nice things for him when I have the money, but I do not want him to think I take him for granted and expect this type of thing from him. But at the same time, what does this say about me? It is not a good thing to know that if he decided to walk out of my life tomorrow, I would die somewhere on a street corner," is how I ended my monologue.

It was just like me to get very dramatic in situations like this. Fortunately, part of the job description as best friend is to talk each other off the ledge, a role Ayesha played very well when I needed her to.

"This is not depressing for many reasons," she answered.

"You have just realized that being with a guy who has money allows you to spend your money on the things you need to spend your money on: paying off debt, lunch in the city everyday, and mani-pedis. The only thing that would change if you and James broke up tomorrow would be what you spend your money on."

"You would not be out on the street. You have your own apartment. You would just have to budget a little more and spend money on groceries rather than Chinese food, and you would have to pay for your own drinks verses random pedicures. It would suck for a little while, but you would be okay—it always works out!" she finished on a high note. It was just what I needed to hear.

As poor as Ayesha and I felt that we were, we had stopped doing shifts at our part-time. It was not our fault, though. We worked for a group of people who were able to pay us based on the number of donations they got the month prior and we had just entered the season when more people were passing out flyers and getting petitions signed so there were fewer people on the phones asking for money. So it was only a matter of time before Ayesha and I started eating into their bank account a little too much.

We were not as upset as they were, though. They had come to really like us. We were their "in" to the young people. The average age of the people there was about fifty years old. They looked forward to the stories we had when we got to work. Truth be told, they were the first ones to recommend that I even write the book you are reading right now. But for Ayesha and me, it was a way out of something we did not enjoy doing without anyone being able to blame us. We didn't quit and we didn't get fired; it was a mutual break up—the best kind.

Chapter 8

Wall Street:
You Can't Do This Forever

There are two types of women in New York. When you are out on that great first date and you are having that great first date conversation about where you work and live and the man says, "I am an investment banker" the first woman hears: "I have a very important job on Wall Street and I make great money and I probably have a great apartment in the city. Date me, date me."

But the second type of woman hears: "Run far, far away!"

Here is the deal about investment bankers: They work! Everything is work. They have breakfast meetings, they have coffee meetings, they have lunch meetings, they have dinner meetings, they have to be available at all times to go into the office, you never see them, and then once you fall in love and really start to value the Saturday and Sunday morning sleeping-in time, they have to get up and go into the office for a conference call. But by then what can you do? You already love him and you are determined to be the understanding girlfriend.

It was April 2006. James and I had been together for almost a year and I decided that for my birthday that year, I wanted to go away and I wanted him to go away with me. My birthday is on April 26th and I started planning for the trip in February. I thought about all the places I wanted to go, where I could afford, and how it would work with James's crazy schedule. I called him to start planting the seed. "Would you go to Puerto Rico with me for my birthday?" I asked one day on the phone while we were both at work.

"Of course I would love to go to Puerto Rico with you. When were you thinking about going?" he asked.

"In a perfect world I would like to leave the day after my birthday," I said. My birthday was on a Wednesday that year and I figured if we left Thursday and came back Sunday, that would be a perfect long weekend and neither of us would have to take too much time off work— just two days.

"Well, you know how my schedule is," he said right off the bat. "Why don't we just play it by ear and see how it looks closer to April. I don't want to disappoint you and have to cancel the trip," he said with nothing but honesty in his voice.

James was trying to make sure I knew he really wanted to go, but something might come up on the job that would hinder him from doing that. But what he didn't understand was the price difference between booking a trip for two to Puerto Rico in February for April, versus booking it in April for April. I might not have the money in April. I barley had the money now. I had the room on my credit card. I had to take advantage of it while I had the money and tickets were cheap.

"I have faith that everything will work out and be fine," I said to him after thinking it through for exactly half a second.

"You will take two vacation days. They can't tell you that you can't take your vacation," I said.

"Okay. But just make sure you get the insurance on the trip so that if we have to move the dates or cancel it, we are able to do that without any penalty," he said. That was great advice—advice he should have told me that morning before I booked the trip.

So it was done. We had a trip booked for two to Puerto Rico leaving April 27th and coming back April 30th with no insurance. February passed and then March passed and then came April (in case you are unsure of the order of the months). I would sporadically ask James for updates on his schedule, all the while fearing that I had booked a five hundred dollar trip and was going to lose all that money. Money I never had in the first place.

Finally it was the second week of April and I needed an update. James had a deal closing on April 24th, the Monday of my birthday week. He would have to work double overtime to get it done so that by Thursday no one would say anything about him having two days off. As Monday the 24th approached, it became clear that the deadline might not be met.

We had to come up with a plan and do it quick. The week prior to the deadline, James started going to work coughing and looking a mess on purpose. All to give the illusion that he was sick. He would stay late and get his work done while getting "sicker and sicker." That Friday before we were scheduled to leave he even had a doctor's appointment. When he went back to work he lied and said that the diagnosis was mononucleosis—otherwise known as mono. He said the doctor told him that it was brought on by being overworked and overstressed. He was very tired and barely had any appetite, but he would continue to go to work and make sure that this deal was done and done on time. April 24th arrived and the deal was done. James was a hero. He had worked through his "mono" and got the work done without complaining or making mistakes. People at his work were practically begging him to take some time off, so he obliged. Puerto Rico was a blast.

Relationships are difficult things. Basically you are telling someone you are going to stand by their side and live life next to them. You are also going to spend time with them, eat with them, see each other at your best, see each other at your worst, agree with each other, disagree with each other, and through it all, still stick with each other because you are in a relationship and that is what it is about. You can't just leave if you are having a bad day or are annoyed with the world; that would mean you are giving up on the relationship. The key is finding someone you can go through all these things with and have it feel like no work at all, just like breathing. But every relationship is going to have something that puts a strain on it. For James and me, it was a combination of his job and our long-term goals.

We were going great. We could spend hours together just lying in bed talking or strolling casually through Brooklyn. We went to some of the best restaurants in New York, watched movies, and cooked dinner for each other at home. We enjoyed countless bottles of great wine and the good times just kept coming and coming. It seemed like this is how it would always be.

There were some weekends that I spent without him because there was a big deal that he needed to close by noon that Tuesday and everyone was going to be at work all weekend. That was not the hard part. I could deal with his crazy schedule because I knew that if he had it his way, he would be at home with me enjoying our time together. My problem was that I was falling in love with this man who treated me like a queen and made me laugh and showed me that I could have a best friend in a boy-friend again. But he didn't want to get married again—not to me—not to anybody! James was then almost thirty-four years old and had been separated from his ex-wife for almost four years and divorced for about a year on paper. When he was twenty and she was nineteen, they had been dating for almost a year and she was five months pregnant. They got married in the basement of a church with no windows in a suburb of Chicago and had a boom box for a band. If you are wondering how I know all of these details, I of course talked in length to my man about his past relationships, as well as my own. But truth also is, I found a vid-eotape of the nuptials in his apartment one day. I will never forget that evening. It started off like any other weekday night where I would get to James's place before he would. I would clean up a little, check my emails on my big-ass, old-school blackberry, figure out what kind of food we wanted to order for dinner and then lounge and watch television until he came home. This evening, I found myself particularly intrigued by the mess of things that lived on top of his refrigerator. There were papers that seemed to be print-outs from work, junk mail he was never getting around to throwing away, an old jewelry box from the seventies that had a gold chain in it that I would later learn belonged to his dad before he passed away, and a video tape that was clearly labeled, 'Our Wedding.'

Immediately I knew I wanted to watch it and I was going to figure out how to watch it—and since VCRs were extinct by this point, I decided to do some digging and see if I could find a company that could convert a VHS to a DVD—and of course, I found one that night. The premise of their business was taking any piece of content that lived on an older format and converting it to a modern one. And in this space in time, it was a DVD. So I packaged it up, labeled it accordingly and sent it in. I honestly can't remember if I asked or told James I was doing this before I got all of the logistics out of the way. Either way, the only question he had was, "Why do you want to watch this?" The real answer was that I was so curious, there was no way I couldn't, so that's what I told him.

It took a couple of weeks, but when it finally showed up in the mail, what a fun night I had by myself at home with my wine, popcorn, and tissues while he was at work! It was everything and nothing I expected: Early nineties horrible ruffles, a much younger version of James, a depressingly not fun reception and the thing I was not ready for, my boyfriend kissing and literally 'being with' another woman. I could handle all of the rest of it, but watching him dedicate his life to this woman and say those vows and seal it with a kiss, was honestly hard to watch. But I got over it, made him watch it with me when he got home, and we had a good laugh about it.

As you can probably agree, getting married to someone after knowing them less than a year while still being a child, who is carrying a child, is not the best decision to make. As they grew into adults and became closer to the versions of themselves they wanted to be, they grew further and further apart. She could not understand, or appreciate for that matter, who she was married to. James, still to this day, is one of the smartest people I know and has knowledge about things that most people run from. He is the most educated, honored, and celebrated human being I know in person (so far) and I decided a long time ago never to take it for granted. From a very young age James decided to put his gifts to good use in any way he could. His ex-wife thought the exact opposite. "Just fine" was just fine with her and working hard to be better, bolder or stronger was a negative in her opinion. That combined with trying to raise children together, maintain some kind of sex life, and be successful in life was James's idea of what marriage and family life should be. Because of this, there were many times during that phase of our relationship that he would remind me that he never wanted to get married again or have any more kids. It was just not for him, and marriage was just a contract.

This issue would come up every now and then in our relationship. Things would be going great. Then we would be at dinner and he would get that look on his face and I knew what was coming. It was the conversation warning me that we were getting too close and why would a twenty-four year old like me love a thirty-three year old like him who had been married for ten years and has three kids. Why would I want to be with him? Why don't I want to find some twenty-eight year old with no kids and no ex-wife and start the perfect life with him? It would end in tears in the restaurant and with me thinking that this man was going to break my heart worse than what I felt in that moment if I didn't get up and walk out of that restaurant and didn't look back. I was going to want way more out of this one day if it stayed as wonderful as it was and from what he was saying, he never would. If it was an episode of *Sex and the City*, Carrie would have walked out of dinner with Mr. Big. But I couldn't. I just had one question for him that he never could answer: how do you know what you are going to want for the rest of your life?

One night at dinner it was just too much to take and I'd had enough. I was not going to let him do this to me. It started like all the other conversations.

"Why do you love me?" he asked me.

"Are you serious?" I replied.

I'd made dinner at his house and we'd just put the food on the table.

"Why are you doing this to me right now?" I asked him. I was not ready for another round of this.

"I am not doing anything to you. I just want to know," was his response.

"Fine. I love you because you are an amazing person. You make me laugh. We have so much fun together doing stupid shit like looking out of the window or sitting on a park bench overlooking the Promenade. Why do you love me?" I turned it back on him.

"You are the one who is amazing," he said without a thought. "You take such great care of me and we are wonderful together," he added.

I cut him off. "So what is the problem?" I asked, I'm sure with an eyebrow in the air. "You start to freak out on me about every three months and I think you don't like the feelings you are feeling for me," I told him.

At this point, I had nothing to lose. We were either going to have this out and have this be the last time we had this conversation, or it was going to be our last conversation. I was serious. I did not want to be in this same place five years from then, and I could tell that was the direction we were headed.

"That is not it at all," he answered. "I love you—I just…You want to get married, I can tell," he said, really in a questioning tone.

I hated that comment for so many reasons. He had no idea. I had dated the same guy for seven years before him and we had just been at the stage of talking about when we would get engaged toward the end of the relationship. I had been with James for a year. Who in their right mind starts talking about marriage after dating for a year? Oh yeah, James and his ex-wife.

I went for honesty without hurtfulness. "Yes. I want to get married," I said. "One day. Not today, not tomorrow, not next year or in the next few years. I don't even know if I want to marry you. Just like I don't need you to know if you want to marry me right now. What I do need you to know is that marriage itself is not completely out of your future if you meet the right woman who makes you happy and you want to spend the rest of your life with her, whether that person is me or not," I said, wanting to yell but maintaining my calm as my chicken got cold. This was something I had said to him many times before. This was never going to end. I could feel the tears coming from the back of my throat.

"I understand what you are saying, Farissa," he said after a few seconds of important silence.

I loved when he said my name. Just something about the way it sounded coming out of his mouth.

"I just don't know the answer to that question right now," he continued. "I don't know if I will ever want to get married again, even if I meet the right woman," he said, punching me in the heart.

That was it. There was nothing I could do. He had made up my mind for me. I had to leave. Was I willing to gamble and stay in this relationship, fall deeper and deeper in love, just for the answer to his question to be no, he never wants to be married?

The answer was "no" in my head and "yes" in my heart. My brain was telling me to get up and get on the train and go home, but my body stayed.

"So then why I am even here? Why are we doing this? This is just a waste of my time," I said. I was so mad and hurt. What we had was so wonderful.

"Are you leaving me?" he asked.

"Yes!" I said in the strongest voice I could muster. "We don't want the same things. Why would I stay with you knowing that my heart is going to be broken in the end?" I asked.

I could tell he didn't want me to leave. But I wanted to. I had to! Instead I left in the morning after we made love.

That weekend all I could do was cry and cry some more. I called my mom and cried with her. I called Ayesha and cried with her. I got my hair done and cried some more. It was the worst I had ever felt. Was it the right decision? How could I break up with someone I love and have a great open, honest relationship with? It didn't make sense to me. James called, but I couldn't talk to him until Monday, mostly because I had no idea what I wanted to say. I had to be on my guard.

"Have you been ignoring my phone calls?" he asked when he finally managed to get me on the phone Monday morning at work.

"Not really," I answered, "just thinking about everything that is going on. What do you want?" I was very interested in what he had to say.

"Well you know that I am traveling on business tonight to Detroit and will be back tomorrow. Can we have dinner tomorrow night when I get back?" he asked me.

I knew there was no way that James would invite me to dinner just for nothing after the weekend we had. He must have something significant to say, and there was no way I could talk about it at work. I could feel the tears coming on already.

"Sure," I answered.

"What time do you get in?" I asked.

After discussing the details it was set. I would meet him in front of his office at eight p.m. tomorrow night.

It was Tuesday. I put on the sexiest, black, work-appropriate dress I had in my closet. James called me when he landed in New York to let me know we were still on and he couldn't wait to see me. I got to his office at eight p.m. on the dot. He came downstairs and he was on his cell phone. He was talking to someone about how the meeting went in Detroit and who was there, what they said, and how the VPs reacted in New York when he told them the news. We got in the cab and he gave the driver the address. I still had no idea where we were going for dinner, but I really didn't care because it's New York, how bad could it be? He finally got off the phone and I could tell he was excited. He was still high from his meeting that had gone really well. I was listening attentively like someone who cared about him. He finally took a breath, so I asked, "Where are we going?"

"Oh, one of the guys at work told me about this really nice place at ground level of one of the hotels in Tribeca. They said it is really good and we should try it," he said.

"Oh okay, sounds good," I said still wondering what tonight was really about.

He was confused and was looking out the window helping the driver find where we were going. He finally saw something he was looking for and we stopped and got out. We walked into the restaurant. It was booming with excitement. I found the hostess stand and stood there waiting for someone to walk up so we could get a table. James kept walking into the dining room, so I followed.

"Where are you going? Don't we need to talk to the hostess?" I asked, a little annoyed and confused because he was acting like he was looking for somebody and I just knew there was no way that could be the case. We turned into the dining room and I heard a guy yell out, "Larry, over here." I turned and looked and there was a table of six people in the back holding two seats for us. My heart dropped to the floor and I wanted to turn and run out the door crying all the way back to Brooklyn. But I swallowed hard and walked up to the table.

There were introductions and I learned very quickly that James was still referring to me as his girlfriend and that this group of people was a group from work. He had been thinking about changing groups and this was the group he wanted to be apart of. So dinner started and there was wine for everyone, two appetizers for each person, dinner that lasted for- ever, then dessert, then after-dinner drinks. The whole time I was on my most perfect behavior. While I was raging with anger and frustration, wanting nothing more then to get up and leave. On the outside, I was making jokes with the boss, telling him how cute his new baby was, and agreeing when he said I was way too beautiful and nice to be with Larry. You would have thought there was nothing wrong. In true investment banker style, we each had a black car waiting for us outside after dinner to take us to our respective homes. We were outside saying our goodbyes and James asked, "Are you coming home with me?"

I gave him a look that must have chilled him to his bones because all he could say was, "What is wrong?"

"What is wrong?" I repeated incredulously. "Get in the car and I will tell you. Driver, 140 Willow," I commanded. That was James's house.

I let him have it. "Let me just start out by informing you that I am very upset, just so that there is no confusion. We just broke up this past weekend and I have felt nothing but utter sadness for the past few days. Then you call me and ask to go to dinner. Excuse me for thinking that it would just be the two of us."

You were the one who said you wanted to talk. Did you not think it was important to let me know that there would be six people waiting for us at the restaurant?" I asked.

"I did…" he tried to talk but there was no way he was taking the reins on the conversation just then.

I cut him off before he could get out another word. "No, you didn't. I asked you where we were going and you told me some place that people at work told you about, not that they would be there waiting for us. When did this all happen, anyway?

"I spoke to you just hours before we met and we were still on, just the two of us. If plans had changed, then that was the time that I should have been informed," I continued, stopping to inhale.

"I'm sorry," he said.

"They saw me right before you arrived, and told me where they were going and that I should come out with them. I told them I was having dinner with my girlfriend and that we hadn't seen each other in a while and they told me to bring you," he explained.

"Since when did you stop thinking for yourself? It is a simple thing to say NO, maybe next time," I said like a mother.

"But you know that I am not happy with the group that I am in and I want to transition into this one. I had to use the opportunity to talk with them and have the team get to know me," he tried to justify.

"And that is the only reason why I didn't act the way I felt in that restaurant tonight," I said. "I wanted to crack your skull open. I know that this was important to you, but our relationship is important to me and if this came up at the last minute, I would have understood and we would have said we will talk at home after dinner. All I am asking for is the common courtesy of being informed of the situation I am walking into. I feel like I am just along for the ride with you sometimes. You make your decisions in your head and don't tell anyone and the rest of the world has to find out on your time. That is not how I operate and that is not how I handle my relationships. We are a team and we are supposed to act like one. If the job of the night is to make these people want to hire you, then that is the job, but I have to KNOW!" I kind of yelled.

I was so mad I could feel my cheeks getting hot and red.

We were almost to his house and I didn't even want to stay there. It was almost midnight and there was no way I was getting on a train as upset and drunk as I was. We walked upstairs and sat on the couch. The cigarette I lit felt like the best cigarette of my life. I took a deep breath in and held it for a moment before I let the smoke escape my lungs and mouth. I was at a loss for words.

"I love you, Farissa," he said.

There goes my name again.

"And I am sorry that I didn't tell you what was going on. I thought I told you in the cab where we were going and what was going on, but I was so excited that I spaced out," he started kissing me.

"I'm sorry," he said.

"I'm sorry," he said again.

"I'm sorry. Do you forgive me?" he asked.

"Stop!" I said. "I am so hurt right now I can't even speak."

We sat there in silence for what seemed like an eternity.

His living room was dark and the only light we had to see each other by was from the street lamps outside of the window and the orange glow of our cigarettes as we inhaled.

"If you think that I want to live the rest of my life alone, you are wrong," he began. "If you think that I want to grow old and watch my kids grow up by myself, I don't. I want someone to share the rest of my life with and I love you. You make me feel like no one else has ever made me feel and the thought of me hurting you tears me up. I don't want to do that. I can see myself with you forever. I just need time—time to figure out what that means for me and what that means for us," he said after I could take no more silence.

My face was a mess. The tears were coming faster than I could wipe them and I could barely see.

"We have time," I said.

"We have all the time in the world to be with each other. I just don't want you to put rules on it like 'this will definitely not happen' or 'that will definitely not happen.' Let's just say that we will play it by ear and let fate do what it does best and whatever happens, happens," I said with tears running down my face in between sobs.

"I love you," he said, "and whatever happens, happens."

And just like that, we were back together.

It had been a few months and we were doing great. Things were open and honest and he was not freaking out. We loved each other, we knew we loved each other, and we were both excited to see what the future had in store for us. James was still working crazy hours and not eating well and coming home at all hours of the morning. One day, it had become just too much.

"I think something is wrong with me," he said as he walked out of the bathroom.

"What is it?" I asked, concerned.

"I just finished going to the bathroom, and there was blood in the toilet," he said.

"What?" I asked. I didn't understand.

"Was it in the water?" I asked.

"No, it was in the crap," he said.

"Well that can't be good. Call your doctor right now and make an appointment," I demanded. Completely disgusted by the topic of our conversation but equally excited that our relationship was at the place where we could.

He did just that. The appointment was in three days, and for the next three days, the situation stayed the same. After the appointment, he called me right away.

"The doctor said that it could be a number of things. But they won't know for sure until they do a colonoscopy," he said.

"What in the world is that?" I asked.

"They have to go inside me and look around and clean it out to get a better understanding of what could have caused it. I have the appointment next week. Will you be able to come with me? The doctor said I will need someone to help me home 'cause I will be drugged," he said.

"Of course! Anything for my boo. And I will do better than that,

I will take you to the doctor, stay with you while you get your colon checked out, and I will still think you are sexy after it's all done," I said.

"Well thank you," he said with an annoyed smirk.

The procedure took about fifteen minutes. The doctor called me back when they were done and James looked drunk and in pain. We sat in the doctor's office as he explained what the problem was. Turns out James had a condition that was not curable. It effects how your food is digested and in what manner it passes through your intestines. The doctor said that this condition normally didn't show itself in men until they were in their forties or fifties. Sometimes it would show up early due to stress and diet. The one thing that James could do to keep it under control moving forward was to take an insane amount of fiber every day. So now, in addition to his blood pressure medicine and vitamins, he had to take about six fiber pills each day. He was not happy.

"This job is killing me slowly," he said once he was sober again. "I have old man problems and I am only thirty-four. This makes no sense. I am always traveling, I am constantly away from my kids, I never see you, and I have to take about eight pills a day just to make all of that happen. What is wrong with this picture?" he asked.

"I know! It sucks. But it is either that or be in pain," I answered.

"I have to make a change. I can't do this forever. I told myself when I got this job that I would only do it for two or three years and then move back to Chicago. I was hoping that I lasted a year and it has been almost three. I have done what I said I would do. Now it is time for me to leave," he said, almost having a conversation with himself.

This wasn't the first time James had talked about moving back to Chicago. He would get all worked up about it in the past and then it would go away and wouldn't come back up again for a while. But now, all the things with work, his health, and how much of his kids' lives he was missing—he was serious. I had told myself that I wouldn't get worked up until he started sending resumes to Chicago. It was that night over dinner when I knew he was serious.

"I really need to get back to Chicago and I am going to start sending out resumes," is how he started the conversation.

"It is October. Hopefully I can start the New Year in Chicago. I think that is a good plan. I have a lot of old contacts that I can look up and start conversations with and see what is going on in the market. This is perfect timing," he explained.

I was sitting there with that supportive look that I give him when I did not know if the plans he was making in his head included me or not. He kept going.

"Kendall will be starting high school next year and I want to be close to him for that, to be able to go to games and be there for prom and all of the important stuff," he said out loud.

Kendall was his oldest son. I could see that James missed his kids.

Everything he was saying was making perfect sense. There was no way I could imagine not being around for all of that stuff for my future kids, so how could I not expect him to want to be around for all of those events for his kids? Frankly, if we were not having this conversation, I would have been worried. He went on and on about how this was the best thing and couldn't wait to start calling all of the right people.

We were done with dinner when he said, "When I move back to Chicago, will you come with me?"

Chapter 9

Brown Guys

While I was in Brooklyn having a relationship, Ayesha was on the Upper East Side trying to maintain her own. Ayesha had fallen hard and quick for Steve and they were in love. They had an unspoken understanding of each other. Steve knew that Ayesha was a princess and he gave her the attention she wanted.

It was a perfect union, except for the fact that she hadn't figured out if it was worth sharing with her family. There was no telling what her family's reaction was going to be when they found out who she was in love with. Her worries were that he was White and not Muslim.

Ayesha often wondered what life would be like if she just found a nice Brown guy to settle down with. It wouldn't be love in the way that she and Steve had, but it would be easier. Her parents would approve, the community she planned on raising her kids in would approve, and her church would approve. It was a choice between true love and convenience.

One of the things that I have always admired about Ayesha is that she can separate her emotions from a situation, more in line with how guys can, and look at things for what they really are. So she decided it was time for her and Steve to have a conversation.

When Ayesha got to work the next day, I knew there was something she needed to tell me. She walked into my office and closed the door. It was still early in the day and I am never all there before ten a.m., so I made sure my coffee was close by.

"So I spoke to Steve last night about how I am feeling about this relationship," she started. "I just don't know how much of a future there is for us. Sometimes I feel like it would be easier if we just broke up."

"Did you say that to him?" I asked.

"No. What I said was 'What do you see happening to us in the future?'"

For some time Ayesha had been hoping that Steve would do something stupid or hurtful that would give her a reason to break up with him. She loved him so much, but there were so many things that made the relationship hard. To Ayesha's discontent, Steve had not come through with delivering any bad behavior. He was as wonderful today as he was when they first got together.

"We spoke really openly about how we feel," she continued. "We talked about our religions and how neither of us is willing to convert and how both of us would want our kids to know our religion and do all of the traditional things we did growing up. So then we had to decide if it would make sense for the kids to be involved in both religions growing up and have them choose when they are older what they want to be," she explained.

"Would they be able to do that?" I asked.

"Well, the only way the kids would be able to come to church with me is if they are part of my sect. So they would have to be…I don't know—it is so confusing. We decided that Steve and his father would go talk to their church and see what our options are and I would do the same. If both of our churches have a solution, we will go with that, but if not, we will have to break up," she said very matter-of-factly.

"Wow! You guys came to this conclusion last night? When will everyone meet with the churches?" I asked.

"As soon as they can get in. I pretty much know what my church is going to say—if you are not Muslim, you cannot participate in any of the ceremonies. We will see. And you know that we have this trip to Aruba planned in a few months," she threw in. They had been planning this getaway for months.

"Oh yeah. What if you guys break up before then? Did you talk about that?" I asked.

"Yeah, we decided that if we had to break up, that trip would be our goodbye. That's how we would say goodbye to each other," she answered.

This was too sad for me to take in. I knew how much Ayesha loved this man and it was crazy to me that two people who loved each other would have to break up over religion.

"Do these churches realize that everyone who believes in religion and God are all praying to the same God, but we just all call him something different and have different traditions of showing him what we believe?" I asked her. "This is the thing I hate about religion. Who are we to tell someone else the way they pray is wrong and the person you have happened to fall in love with cannot spend the rest of their life with you because they choose to show their love for God in a different way? It is so hypocritical!" I preached.

Ayesha agreed with me, but there was nothing she could do. For her, it was about more than staying true to her religion. She had to worry about living up to her parents' hopes and dreams of following in the traditions that they had been a part of for decades. It was something that I couldn't relate to. Although I had grown up in a Christian household and went to church every Sunday of my life until I left Richmond, I always knew that it was not for me and that what we learned in church about how to live life like responsible, loving, giving individuals and the rewards you get for doing so, is true for any person no matter what you believe or whether you tithe ten percent or not. But I tried to understand for my friend.

One of the reasons why it took so long for Ayesha to tell her parents about Steve was because she wanted to make sure she was destroying their world for a reason. What if she told her parents and they were devastated and then she and Steve broke up that following month? She wanted to avoid this type of situation by making sure she and Steve were the real thing. The time finally came when she knew she had to tell them. Due to the stress and guilt this whole thing was causing her, she had to get it off her chest—but it was a matter of how.

It was around November 2006 and Ayesha's mom had decided she was coming to New York to see her daughter and spend some time with her sister who lived in Jersey. Ayesha knew it was a "spy on Ayesha" trip, but there was nothing she could do but go along for the ride. Her mom was coming in on a Saturday and leaving on Monday. Saturday was her day with her mom. They were going out to dinner in the city on Saturday night and then Ayesha's mom was catching the train to Jersey. She told Steve where they were going to dinner and she was off.

Steve, being the hilarious guy that he is, decided to show up at the same restaurant with a couple of guy friends of his and sit at the bar to have a few drinks. Ayesha saw him walk in and her whole being froze up. She was so nervous she couldn't even look at him. The entire time they were making noise and being loud on purpose. At one point, Ayesha's mom even noticed them in the corner and glanced over. Ayesha couldn't wait for this horrible night to be over. She made it through with flying colors and as soon as she could get Steve to herself, she let him have it.

"What were you doing tonight? That was crazy. Do you know how nervous you made me? I'm surprised my mom didn't ask me what the hell was wrong with me," she scolded.

"I just wanted to see what my love's mom looked like and what you will look like when you get old," Steve said, a little drunk from his night at the bar.

"Your mom is beautiful. I'll be fine," he finished.

When a guy says things like that to you, how can you be mad?

"Well, lucky for you she didn't figure anything out," was all she could think to say.

"Hey, why don't you tell your mom next time you are in Dallas: 'Mom, remember that guy who was up at the bar the night we went to dinner? Well he is my boyfriend and I love him and I want to be his wife,' and just see what she says."

Ayesha figured that at this point it couldn't be any worse than tonight.

That Monday, we had a brainstorming session of the best way to tell her parents the news. There were plenty of ideas thrown out there because there were so many people interested in this situation at work. People, including my boss, would check in with Ayesha periodically just to ask her if she'd told her parents yet. It was very annoying and stressful, even for me. Everyone had an opinion and they wanted theirs to matter. Didn't they get that mine was the only one that counted? Ha! People had ideas like: just tell them, or write them a letter and mail it, or have him come with you to Dallas and tell them when you are on the way, or send them a card. In the end, it was way too much stress and it needed to be done. One weekend Ayesha flew down to Dallas to spend it with her friends and decided to tell her mom the truth. There were tears and questions and words. At the end of the conversation, Ayesha's mom did say that she wanted her to be happy, but she wanted all the normal things for her, too, which included her marrying a nice Pakistani man there in Dallas with the whole community invited. All she could say was, "We won't tell your father yet, and we will just see what happens." That was enough for Ayesha!

In the midst of all of this, Ayesha's religion didn't stop being important to her. She continued to go to her Religious Center in the city and meet other young Pakis like herself who lived in New York and knew exactly what she was going through.

One Friday night she decided to go to a new church that had just opened for her sect. It was great! She walked in and it was full of Pakis in their twenties. Every man in there would have been acceptable to her parents. Her man was not even allowed to set foot inside the church.

Afterwards, everyone was socializing when Ayesha heard someone call her name.

"Ayesha. Do you remember me?" asked the voice.

Ayesha turned around to see a really cute guy walking toward her. He had on a great suit, he had obviously just come from work, and he was very well-groomed. Ayesha remembered his face, but couldn't remember where she knew him.

"I went to Southern Methodist University," he said to try and jog her memory. At that moment she remembered. His name was Rasheed and she had hung out with him a couple of times in college in Texas. They met at a couple of parties and went out for drinks at a bar with a group of friends about four years ago.

"Hi Rasheed, I do remember you," she said. "What are you doing here?" she asked.

"After school I moved to New York for work. I am an investment banker at Morgan Stanley," he explained.

We couldn't get away from them! From our perspective, New York is crawling with investment bankers. They stayed and talked for a while after the service and caught up on life. For some reason Steve never came up once. At the end of the conversation, Rasheed wanted to know if Ayesha would ever want to go have a drink after work. She said yes without hesitation. She would figure out how that would work later—or that next afternoon on the phone with me.

That next day we spoke about it but I couldn't give too much advice because James was on the couch next to me the entire time and he and Steve had become friends, naturally. So I couldn't take any chances. Even though they never hung out with just the two of them, they both worked on Wall Street and would run into each other often. It was too dangerous. I told Ayesha I would think about it and let her know something on Monday (because there was no texting yet), and in the meantime she was not to do anything stupid.

As with many of the obstacles that came our way during our friendship, the solution was generated over morning coffee.

"Here is the deal," I said. "You love Steve and he loves you. You guys are having a great time right now and you can see yourself with him forever. You also know that there are some things that you will have to deal with if you guys do get married which you don't know if you are willing to put up with—from your family, from society, and just stupid people. With this guy, you see something that, if it worked out, would be the perfect situation for you. You know my motto in life: You never want to leave a situation behind and years later wonder what would or could have happened. So my advice is to have drinks with him. Not by yourself, but with a group of your girls, too, so there is no temptation or foul play. I know that this goes against my rule of not doing anything you don't want your man to do, but you owe this to yourself!"

Ayesha knew I was right.

"If you think about it, this is just how I met James," I continued.

"If I had not taken the chance and met him for the weekend to see if I could even stand him, I would have missed out on true love. Who knows, you guys could meet and talk and he could turn out to be the biggest ass in the world. The only rule we have to put on it is that you can't call him to set up drinks. If he calls and wants to hang out, I will drop what I'm doing to meet you and we will test it out together," I said, putting a bow on the discussion.

It was done. The rules were set and we were going to let fate take care of the rest. In the next couple of weeks, Rasheed called and they would try to get together, but whenever we were going out, he couldn't and when he wanted to go out, it was too much like a date, requesting Friday or Saturday nights, which was time that was set aside for the boyfriends. They saw each other in church a couple more times and three months later, still hadn't spoken to each other. I guess that is what fate wanted.

It was finally time for Ayesha and Steve to go to Aruba.

They had been waiting for this vacation for quite a while. There had been no meetings with any churches or priests. They knew what the answers were going to be and they didn't want to hear it. They loved each other and that was all that mattered. They would deal with things as they came. If Ayesha's family knew about them, they would be disappointed, but Steve's family had accepted her a long time ago, so it was just time to live life and see what happened.

Aruba was great. They ate, drank, and laid in the sun for a week straight. They came back with great tans, highlighted hair, and deeper in love than before. It was almost sickening. I was very happy for Ayesha. Things were great for both of us. We both had men that loved us and wanted to be with us. We were both having conversations about the future with them.

It was fourth quarter so we would be negotiating our new salaries in a few weeks. We had both made our budgets and we were on top of the world. We both had our best friend at our side. Christmas was nearly there, what could be better? Needless to say, when things are this perfect, something is bound to happen to shake your world. We didn't know it at the time, but our earthquake was right around the corner.

Chapter 10

Conclusion?

It was December 2006. I had been back in New York for fourteen months. Where had the time gone? It is so funny. Time takes its time while you are in the middle of experiencing it, but when you look back, it really goes by quickly. It had been a great year. What was 2007 going to bring me? Only time would tell...

James was still posting resumes and talking to people about going back to Chicago. He asked me months ago if I would move to Chicago with him and I had said yes right on the spot without hesitation. I knew that I owed it to myself to see where this relationship would take me. Trying to find a new job was a slow process for James. These big businesses deal with big money, so when they look at bringing in people to work for them, they take the hiring process very seriously. I was not upset, though. It just postponed his move and me having to deal with the issue of when I would move to Chicago, how I would find a job, and if I was ready to be a stepmom. I loved him and if he was not going to be in New York, then no matter how much I loved the city, I didn't want to be there, either.

We had worked out a plan. When he got a job in Chicago, he would go out there and get things set up, find us a place to live, get his feet wet with work. Then I would come out there to visit, interview with a couple of places, either within my company or decide to go back to local radio sales, and make the move about six to twelve months later. I was comfortable with the decision and the way it would all work out. We were happy. I just wanted it to happen later rather than sooner because I was having so much fun, and this was the first time in my life that I had such a great friend that I could count on completely and be one hundred percent myself with. I was not ready to give that up so fast.

Ayesha was not that happy about the plan, either. She was happy for me and knew that she would do the same thing if Steve had to move somewhere else, but we still had to prepare ourselves for what we knew was coming. I was going to move to Chicago!

It was December 22nd and Christmas was only a few days away. It was annual season so we were all busy. It's when the larger agencies that buy advertising for the larger companies plan out their budgets for the year and try to buy up as much inventory as possible at a reduced, upfront price. Advertisers try their best to plan their paid media buys across the country for the following year so that they get a good deal and only have to worry about adjusting things as need be as the year goes on. It was great because it was motivation to make money for 2007.

The better I did at negotiating the annual agreements for 2007, the more money I knew I would get my president to agree to pay me for the next year. It was very exciting.

My sales team was the only one in the office that day. Our director of sales was having surgery on one of the clogged arteries in his heart and our president was out in San Francisco visiting some of our client radio stations. It was almost lunchtime when my phone rang.

"Hello? Farissa? It's Mike." It was my president calling from San Francisco. This was weird because he never called me from New York, so it had to be serious if he was calling me from San Francisco.

"Where is everyone?" he wanted to know.

"Matt is in here with me and Tom is probably downstairs having his before-lunch smoke. Why? What's wrong?" I asked.

"I just need to talk to everyone together. Can you do me a favor and gather everyone together and give me a call back on my cell phone?" he asked.

"Okay we'll give you a call back when Tom gets upstairs," I answered.

He hung up and I was so confused. What could it be? We had been in negotiation with our stations to extend their contracts with our company so that we could continue to rep them for five or six more years. We had often joked that Mike would call a meeting one day and say we were all fired because the stations had gone to the competition, but we never really thought it would happen. Mike kept us informed and the last time we all spoke he said the news was that the higher-ups were telling him there was no reason for us to be worried about losing the stations. We were doing a great job and unless something drastically changed, he didn't see a need for a change in our situation. So what could it be?

Tom finally came back upstairs yelling at me that I never came down to join him. I told him what Mike had said when he called and that we needed to call him back immediately. They all came in my office and I dialed Mike on speaker.

"Hello?" he answered.

"Hey Mike, it is all of us. We are in my office," I said.

"Okay, I am on my cell phone and I just walked into the Interep office in LA. Let me call you guys right back on the land line." He hung up again and we waited anxiously.

"What do you guys think it is? Are we getting pink slips?" I asked.

"I don't know," Tom replied. "What about Frank?" he asked.

"That's right. I completely forgot that Frank's surgery was today. They were going into his heart to clean it up. What if something happened to him on the table and he died? Oh my God!" I started freaking out. My phone rang.

"Hey Mike," I answered.

"Hey guys. Is the door closed?" he asked.

"Yeah, and we are all here," I answered.

"I wanted you guys to hear this from me. The station group called me this morning right after I landed in LA to tell me that they have decided to take the stations over to the competition. They thought long and hard about the decision and it was not a performance issue or anything like that because we did a fucking awesome job for them. The growth we had from 2005 to 2006 was the highest percentage of growth they had ever seen with these stations. They were just able to get a better commission rate from the competitor and it made the shareholders happier. It was much more of a corporate decision," he explained in his thick Queens accent.

While Mike was talking, we were all kind of staring at each other in disbelief. When Mike was done, he opened the floor for questions. We turned to Matt because he was always the one with questions.

"So when does this go into effect?" he asked.

"I know that all three of us have annuals up right now for a lot of the stations. Do we keep working on them or what?" Matt finished.

"It goes into effect immediately," Mike answered. "Stop selling the stations. Contracts are going to be sent over to their new company starting tomorrow morning. It will be up to their new reps to call the buyers and let them know that they have these stations now. From what I hear, some of them have already started," Mike continued.

This was too much to take in.

"So what do you want us to do in the meantime?" I asked.

"Well, I will be back in New York tomorrow," he said. "I wish they had told me this news before I flew to California to meet with stations! Anyway, in the meantime, I want you guys to call some of the buyers you have worked with over the years and let them know what is going on so they hear it from us first. Do not submit on anything anymore, and we will have a meeting when I get back into town," he finished.

The feeling I felt was a mixture of too many things. I was very glad that it was not news about Frank dying on the table.

But once I was done being happy that Frank was still alive, I was in disbelief. I didn't have a job and Christmas was around the corner. A new year was around the other corner and I had to look for another job. I had to talk to Ayesha!

"WHAT!" That is all Ayesha could say.

"I know, but don't tell anyone yet. I am not even supposed to be telling you," I told her.

"So what does that mean for you? What about your money? Are you still going to get paid?" she asked.

"We spoke to Mike some more this afternoon and he said that the company has agreed to pay us until the end of the year, which is two weeks away, and help us find a job within the company, whether it be in the New York office or an outer office."

For those who have been with the company for a while and don't find a job by the end of the year, they will get two weeks pay for every year they have been with the company," I explained as if I was reading from a manual.

Ayesha just sat there and took in the whole story just as I did from Mike on the phone. Even as I repeated it, it didn't sound real to me. Could this really be happening now? Everything had been going so well. After another moment of silence, Ayesha finally gathered her thoughts together enough to say, "I guess you are moving to Chicago."

Christmas was here! James had decided that it would be a good idea for us to fly to Richmond for a couple of days before the holidays for him to meet my parents. Yes, ladies and gentlemen, James had finally decided. So we went down there and he met a lot of my friends from high school, friends from my old job, and most importantly, he met my family. We all went to church together on Christmas Eve and I made a big dinner for everyone at my dad's house. We had a flight back to New York that evening because we wanted to wake up on Christmas morning in each other's arms at home in Brooklyn, just the two of us. It was the best Christmas I had ever had!

After that, it was time to get to work on finding a job. I had talked to James to see how serious he was about moving to Chicago. I wanted to know when he saw himself moving there because if he was serious and if he wanted to do this now, I would see if my company would transfer me out there to work for a different group. It would be a good situation. One of the girls that I worked with at the radio station in Richmond was now a director of sales for the group that Bruce ran. The same lady who had made the email introduction for me to Bruce! She now lived in Chicago, was running a department for Bruce, and needed to add someone to her team. Because Bruce had hired me into the company, ran the Rapper program, and was my best friend's boss, I knew I wouldn't have a problem getting him to see if he could afford to send me to Chicago. James said he was serious and that he was sure that he would have something soon. So I decided that I would talk to Bruce about moving me out to Chicago.

In the meantime, I couldn't put all of my eggs into one basket just in case Bruce didn't come through. So I decided to interview with some other places in New York and Chicago. I interviewed at the number one Clear Channel (now iHeart) radio station in New York. I interviewed for a position with the company that picked up the radio stations that Interep had just lost, and while I was there, learned that they had a Chicago position, as well. I was busy as hell for those couple of weeks. I had my favorites, but I was also very confused. It was a very stressful time. I wanted to be with James and I wanted to make this move with him to Chicago, but I was torn because I was also interviewing with the number one station in the country and they wanted to hire me. That was not a small thing. This thing with James had better work out because I was giving up a dream job at a top station for the number one media company in the United States, in New York City. This had better be good.

I negotiated with Bruce and accepted the position in Chicago with Interep's network department. Jackie, my ex-coworker from Richmond, was going to be my boss and the company was going to pay for me to move out there. It was almost perfect. But I was leaving Ayesha. The next few weeks were really sad.

It was the week after New Year's and it was officially 2007. I had a job waiting for me in Chicago, which I was going to start on February 5th, but until then I was off work and still getting paid. Now it was time for me to say goodbye to my friends. For the next few weeks I would wake up late, go into the office a couple days a week to have lunch with Ayesha and the rest of my friends or come up after work and go to happy hour with them. I was also involved in sorting out the move with the company and making sure I was available for the moving company when they needed to put together an estimate for billing.

One of those weekends, James and I flew to Chicago to look at apartments and pick one out for us to live in. Things were moving right along. I had a job with a raise, my man was going to meet me in Chicago in our new two-bedroom apartment in the South Loop, and I was in love. The only problem was that I was leaving Ayesha.

We were down to the last week and Ayesha and Stephanie had every day of that week planned out with some fun activities for us to do in one last attempt to say goodbye. For my last full weekend in the city, the girls decided it would be a good idea to go to brunch. It was nice because I was not used to seeing them on the weekends, so for Ayesha and I to leave the boyfriends on a Sunday was a big deal. This was not just any brunch though, it was a drag queen brunch where you got first class entertainment from some of the best drag queens in the city. They poured us bottomless glasses of mimosas and lip-synced to songs like "I Will Survive." It was great. We left there drunk and happy we were not lesbians.

On Monday I was ordered to come up to the office and have lunch with all my office friends. We ate and talked and I answered all the questions that I hated like: are you going to miss Ayesha? Has James found a job? What is your apartment like? What are Matt and Tom doing? It was all so very ceremonial. But I did it and then went and had dinner with my sister that night.

The next two days were all-night-long happy hours. I can taste the vodka tonics just thinking about it. We went to a bar that we frequented near the office and spent way too much money. One of those nights was just me and Ayesha and then the next night she sent out evites to people in the office to come join us. You would have thought we were Paris Hilton and Britney Spears, circa 2007 of course.

For my last night of partying, Stephanie made a reservation for me, herself, Ayesha, and a few other girls we were friends with to have dinner at this awesome sushi place in the city. It was so out of the way I could never find it again, but it was wonderful and it was BYOB. We had bottles and bottles of wine. After dinner, we decided that we wanted the party to keep going. Since we were in Stephanie's part of town, we went to this underground bar where the only thing that exposed its location was a red light on the outside of the door. We stayed there for hours and drank some more and invited more people out. One of our girlfriends from work came out and Ayesha and I even made the boyfriends find us. I went home and threw up, but I had the time of my life with all of my friends in one place. That was the last time I saw Ayesha as a resident of New York City.

It was February 2nd and I was on a one-way flight from New York to Chicago with Buddy Snuggles the cat, enough clothes to get by until my stuff showed up at the new apartment, and memories from the past year. I was very excited to start a new phase of life and see what was waiting for me in Chicago: What friends were waiting to be made and where the relationship with James was going to go? I had so many unanswered questions and lots of time to figure out the answers.

James had a couple of interviews set up for the next few weeks in Chicago, but it was going to be two weeks before I saw him again. That gave me plenty of time to set up the apartment and get things looking the way I wanted, especially for the first time James was to see the apartment. I was starting my job on Monday and I was on pins and needles. Was this really happening? When would I see Ayesha again? Was I really starting over again in a new city? I have moved so many times and have lived in cities that most people only visit on vacation. It was too much to take in.

Two months had gone by. Chicago was shaping up to be a great city. It was cleaner than New York, much more affordable, and then there is Lake Michigan. The weather was—and still is—a bitch, especially if you arrive in February. I do not recommend that at all! The Chicago Interep office was very different than the New York office. There were not as many people on the sales floor. I would say there were about one-third the people in Chicago that were in New York. There were not as many young people there, and the worst part was there were only women in the office.

So you know what that means: a lot of bitches! Cattiness. Mean girls and, unfortunately, perverbial doors closed in my face. I made it past the hard part of being the new girl and made my friends in the office. None of them would ever replace Ayesha, but they were people who I would actually consider talking to after work, so that means something.

It took a little longer than either of us wanted for James to find a new job, but he finally got the position that he wanted as a senior vice president at a boutique investment bank. He was very happy, and on the chilly Chicago night that I wrote this section of the book in late March 2007, he landed from his one-way flight from New York to Chicago.

The summer of 2007 was in front of us and we were looking forward to good times. For a very long time, I talked to Ayesha every day and we missed each other very much. We were constantly online looking at flights to try and catch a cheap one for me to make it back to New York or for her to make it here to Chicago. Some years have now passed, so the frequency of that has definitely slowed down, but we love each other no less.

Sometimes I wish that Ayesha would just move to Chicago with Steve so we all could live happily ever after, but that would just be an easy out for an ending—and although neither of us knew it, this was just the beginning of our stories.

About the Author

Farissa Alexander Knox was born and raised in The Bronx. Attending New York City public school, having international childhood friends, and living in a bubble of inclusion and real diversity are just some of the things she attributes to her view on life today. Eventually attending high school and college in Virginia due to her parents' moving, Farissa majored in Communications and Advertising at Christopher Newport University, graduating in 2003. Jumping straight into her career after school, she spent two years selling advertising in Richmond, Virginia, then moved back to New York to do the same for a few more years. From there, her personal life brought her to Chicago where her career truly blossomed as she took her years of experience selling advertising, along with the relationships developed over that time, and turned it into her first business: RLM Media, a media buying advertising agency and holding company established in 2008, specializing in the Health-care, Political, Recruitment, and Consumer space. Later, she created WhatRUWearing, a digital content publishing house focused on creating engaging, beautiful digital content for brands and platforms who need to talk to today's young woman who loves fashion, style, beauty, and creativity. Farissa currently lives in Chicago's Lake View neighborhood with her husband Larry and two daughters, Chloe and Isabelle.